Chapters

$4 A GAME

That was my first game fee for officiating. Actually the check was for $8 because my first paying assignment was umpiring a men's fast-pitch softball doubleheader. Two games, seven innings, eight-run mercy rule, ASA rules. And I am 15 years old and it is the summer of 1973.

Of course, none of the players were 15 years old. These guys were in their 20's, 30's, 40's, and even 50's. Guys I had known my whole life. Guys that had been playing since my dad umpired. Guys that drank beer between games, smoked cigarettes between innings, worked real jobs during the day, but still believed they could cover the outfield like Mickey Mantle, or run the bases like Lou Brock. Guys that we, as kids, looked up to as local stars.

One of the local teams at the time was the Sterling Merchants and their manager was John Moore. John came to my house on a Wednesday afternoon to see if I would work their games that night. This was long before cell phones, text messages, and email. We had a landline, but there was a good chance that John didn't. I am pretty sure now, some 40 years later, I was not his first choice.

In actuality, I was probably not a choice at all, but a desperate move to keep the game from being canceled. The teams in Sterling played their home games on Wednesday nights. Always did. They played other local teams from similar small towns in the area. Each town had designated home nights. Sterling's was Wednesday.

In fact, John didn't even get to ask me to my face. I was under our house at the time, in a crawl space trying to repair some plumbing that my dad, at 6-7, and about 285 lbs., could not get to. John stuck his head in the opening, which was some 30 feet from where I was lying, and made his pitch. "I know you can do the job," I remembered him saying. "I wouldn't ask you if I didn't think you could."

It wasn't that I hadn't umpired games before. I had. But they were youth league softball games that I was playing in just a year or so before.

You see, fast-pitch softball in Sterling at the time was a big deal, as it was in most small towns during that time. But mainly because, as kids in Sterling, we didn't play Little League baseball, we played fast-pitch softball in the Lial Newman League. To this day, I don't know who Lial Newman was, but I knew in the summer, we were going to play Lial Newman ball.

So I grew up on softball.

I was registered; I had been to the local clinic. I had that triangular, shield-looking, ASA patch on my powder-blue shirt that indicated I was an "Official Umpire". I had seen my dad and many others work those same games every Wednesday night. The ball park in the summer was what I lived for. I had been a bat boy. I chased foul balls for a nickel each. I ran the PA system and kept a scorebook on more occasions than I can remember for all kinds of games. But this was going to be different.

When John left and I finished doing my part under the house, I started getting ready. I'm not sure why or how come, because all I had for umpiring was my blue shirt with the patch and a hat. It wasn't a plate hat, but it was a dark blue hat.

I did not have any protective equipment, but that was available at the ball park. I did not even have a brush to sweep the plate, or a ball bag to keep extra balls. I didn't even have a pair of black shoes. Even at the age of 15, I wore a size 14 shoe, so the outlay for a pair of umpiring shoes was not something I gave much thought.

Double-headers always started at 7 o'clock. And I knew that I was supposed to be at the game site 30 minutes before game time. The park was on the other end of town from our house. More often than not I could get a ride home after the games. I didn't own a bicycle, but remember, this is small-town Kansas in the early 70's. Outside of a few strange dogs, there wasn't much to worry about in making such a trip. So I walked to the park in my uniform, what there was of it.

My usual ride home from the ballpark more often than not came from my first mentor in officiating, Don Butts. Don was a former player-turned-umpire who had some state tournaments under his belt. I'm not sure why he decided to take me under his wing, but Don helped me a lot during those early softball days. We eventually worked a lot together, and many nights we would sit in his car in my parent's driveway discussing the events from that particular night.

I can't say I remember anything in particular about the evening other than I got through it and did have a couple of players come up to me after the game and tell me I did a pretty good job. That felt good, along with an $8 check at the end of the night made out to Dwight Nichols.

Fast-pitch softball is where I got my real start in officiating. For the next few years, until I got out of college, it would be my bread and butter. It took me to a lot of places and introduced me to many people who, over 40 years later, are still part of my life. Outside of basketball for four years in high school and one year in college, I never gave playing sports any real consideration again. Okay, I have since then, but we are a long way from that point.

From this point on, I wanted to be involved in sports as an official.

TIME-OUT

We all have those times in our officiating careers that we look back on and smile. Even laugh. But at the time, smiling or laughing is the last thing on our minds. My first such experience, and most horrifying, occurred just two summers after that first fast-pitch doubleheader.

As I mentioned in the previous chapter, softball in Sterling was a big deal. In addition, along with men's fast-pitch games, there were also girl's teams that played each other in the area, and of course, they needed umpires as well.

These girls' teams played basically the same small towns in the area that the men's teams did, only the home games in Sterling were on Tuesday nights. The Lial Newman League that I mentioned before played on Monday and Thursday evenings.

So on most Tuesdays, I could be found at the same diamond in town working ballgames with players my age as. And for most of the summer, I also made the rounds to towns in the area working girls fast-pitch tournaments for what would progressively grow from $5 per game to $10 per game over the next few years.

During those days, Don, myself, and a third umpire from Sterling, Leonard Detter, would umpire a variety of tournaments on the weekends that would produce a check for somewhere between $100 - $150 per weekend. Do that during the months of June, July, and August and pretty soon it grows into real money for a kid in high school in the early 70's. That tournament money was what I put away for the beginning of school, car repairs, and the State Fair. But the doubleheaders kept me in pocket money for whatever we teenagers needed pocket money for back then.

That brings me back to a particular doubleheader night.

About the only good thing about the whole experience that I am about to describe is that at least it was the second game of the doubleheader. After that, as they say, the rest is history.

At some point in the second game, as I am working the plate, my body begins to send me a message that it is prepared to perform a bodily function we normally sit through. Now remember, I am working the plate, which puts me as close to a sitting position as a person gets without actually sitting down.

I can only imagine that someone at the game that night noticed a change in my plate mechanics to a more upright stance. Needless to say, I knew that wasn't going to last long. Finally, after what seemed like an eternity, the half-inning ended. With that, I laid my mask (my own mask by this time) on home plate, called time-out, and made a mad dash to the restroom.

This dash covered about 50 yards. As luck would have it, a kid younger than me comes out just before I go in. Now this is not just some port-a-potty. It is a cinder-block building with regular plumbing, but still only a "one-holer". The departure of the only other occupant just before I rushed in came at an opportune time. However, besides that, my timing was less than perfect. In fact, it stunk. Pun intended.

I physically made it to the restroom. However, the reason I went there in the first place arrived before I did. Therefore, a majority of my time in there was spent preparing myself for a graceful return to the game. I did return and finish the game. The whole episode took less than 10 minutes, but to those on the field waiting to finish the game, I'm sure it seemed a lot longer.

Everyone knew where I went and what I intended to do once I got there. Until today though, I am not sure how many, if any, know the true details of the results. But I am sure most could guess. You have gotten all of the details out of me you are going to get. Let's just say that the ultimate results were less than desirable and this was one night that couldn't end quickly enough, paycheck or no paycheck.

Thank God nothing like this has ever happened to me again. But I'm sure we have all heard of similar stories involving similar functions or others that we do not care to perform in public. With the thousands of officials out there and the thousands of games of all kinds being played, this kind of thing might happen on a daily basis to someone, somewhere.

I've had my turn.

SCARED TO DEATH

By now, you know that my early years of officiating centered on umpiring softball games played during the summer. And, as you can imagine, an umpire can run across all kinds of situations and opportunities to "make or break" a career.

Though these teams did play to a higher level for the most part, there were those times that bring a person to wonder how some of them managed to make it to the ballpark on time. And there were times that made an umpire wish they hadn't.

A particular Kansas ASA Men's Class A Fast-Pitch State Final was one of those times.

This was around 1980 and was Kansas' first attempt at splitting out some of the lesser teams from the Men's Major Fast-Pitch division. The goal being to increase team participation and provide an avenue for teams to advance to a higher level of play previously reserved for a select few teams.

The tournament was played in the city of McPherson, which had a strong history of girls fast-pitch, but little, if any, history where men's teams were concerned. However, McPherson was centrally located to the hotbeds of the state's men's fast-pitch teams.

Basically, the way it worked, teams would advance to state tournament play through local district tournaments. Depending on the number of teams registered in each district, a specific number of teams advanced to the state tournament.

With the addition of another class of competition, and the way the class system worked initially in Kansas, a district could send its top two or three teams to the Major State Tournament and the next two or three teams to the Class A State Tournament. So 16 teams came together in McPherson for the inaugural Class A State Tournament.

Overall, the tournament drew little attention from the city, the fans, and the players. Most of the teams were just tickled to be there, to still be playing in August.

Many of the teams I had seen before during the course of the summer at the many tournaments I had worked that year and summers before. As was typical for tournaments during this time, games began on Thursday night, with play continuing Friday night, all day Saturday, and into the late afternoon-early evening on Sunday. Weather permitting, of course.

Well, the weather did hold out, and the double-elimination tournament finally worked itself down to the final two teams, Margie's Café of Wichita and the Salina Boosters. Here is where it got scary.

Margie's was a perennial power in the state at the time, having won the state's Major title previously, and led by Kansas ASA Hall of Fame pitcher Billy Ray Jackson. They wound up in the Class A tournament as a result of being upset during the Wichita district. Salina, on the other hand, had some talent, but never really seemed to play well enough together to be a real challenger to the elite teams of the time.

Margie's, obviously disappointed to be in McPherson and not getting ready for the Men's Major scheduled for the next weekend in Topeka, was defeated in their first game of the tournament. That was the wake-up call they needed as they battled all the way through the loser's bracket to make it back to the championship games. Salina was the undefeated team in the tournament and needed to win only one more game to claim the title and advance to the regional.

Now if you have been around adult softball tournaments of any kind you probably have a pretty good idea of how the weekend usually goes. In the beginning, everyone is excited, games go by quickly, and the tournament stays on schedule. By late Saturday, into play on Sunday, the games slow down, teams realize that elimination is near, and the beer begins to flow.

This tournament was no different.

Being only about 30 miles from home, I was asked to stay and work the "if" game of the tournament on the plate. The "if" game is the second game played "if" the undefeated team loses

13

the first championship game. As my luck would have it, Margie's won the first game. They were the better team, and, even though they had played in what seemed like half the games in the tournament, their skill showed.

By now, Salina players began to show their true colors as well. By the time the championship games arrived, even though they continued to win, they also continued to enjoy their barley pop. By Sunday night, they had consumed plenty, and had their lunch handed to them by Margie's in the first championship game.

The second championship game was turning out to be a repeat of the first. In addition, under ASA rules at the time, there was no mercy rule in the championship games. Win by one, win by 20; we are going to play seven innings. It was an ugly seven innings, on the field and under the mask.

The more Margie's scored, the more pissed Salina became. For them, nothing seemed to work, and, of course, the umpires couldn't get any calls right. As the night went on and the innings went by, Salina's displeasure became more evident. They got vocal, they got intimidating, and they got threatening.

Each inning the catcher had something to say. Either to me, about me, about my partner, about what he was planning to do, about what he wanted to do. One of the things he repeatedly told batters as they stepped into the box was that he and the pitcher talked about him ducking a pitch and letting me take one on behalf of his team.

Looking back, we can talk about all the things I should have done. I could have tossed the catcher, and/or the pitcher. Or anybody else that proved to be threatening. I could have stopped the game and made the state umpire-in-chief, who was at the game, do something to help restore some law and order.

I chose to bite my tongue and get the damn thing over with. My partner wasn't much help. He either didn't understand the situation or was hell-bent on showing everyone he belonged in a championship game. Because every situation that needed him to deliver a judgment, he not only delivered it, he delivered it as if he was working a WWE match between Hulk Hogan and Andre the Giant, which only stoked Salina's fire.

I really had no idea what was going to happen at any given time. Would this catcher really duck a pitch? Would one of their batters "accidentally" let his bat go across my forehead? When it ended, you can imagine which side of the field we had to leave from.

In the umpire's trailer afterwards, all I could do was just sit there thinking what in the world had I just been through. My partner was ready with every explanation of what went wrong, why he wasn't part of the problem, and all of the things he should have done. I just sat there, thinking to myself that maybe this wasn't what I really wanted to do. The umpire-in-chief raked us over the coals about the whole situation. I just sat there. Shocked. Scared. Numb.

When it finally looked like it was all clear and most of the potential wrongdoers were gone I beat it out of there, thinking what would next weekend's Major tourney be like? Would I even get the chance to work it? How much of this would precede me?

When I checked into the hotel on the following Thursday, I ran into the state Umpire-In-Chief in the lobby. To his credit, he stepped up and put out his hand. Then he and I both apologized for the events from the previous weekend, knowing we both could have done things better.

Thankfully, since then I have never found myself in anything even remotely like that situation. I was followed out of a baseball park in Lyons, Kansas, one night after a Babe Ruth district game in which I tossed a kid for an f-bomb he delivered to a pitcher while crossing home plate on a wild pitch. The problem was his team, leading by lots, had used all of its substitutes and this kid's ejection left the team ahead with no remaining players. They thus had to forfeit the game, the championship, and the opportunity to advance to the state tournament.

Needless to say, some of the parents who would never believe that "their" kid would ever act like this didn't understand, nor did they care. All they cared about was that their kid's team lost and I was the reason why. A couple of cars followed me out of the parking lot that night, slowly. Nothing came of it. However, under the right circumstances, these kinds of potentially dangerous situations can become a reality more often than any of us would likely care to know. In those instances, all it takes is someone to pour a little gas on the small fire to set the whole situation ablaze.

Fortunately, on these occasions nothing happened, but the gas can was full and the cap was off. All we needed was someone ready to pour. Thank heavens, whoever had that can in their hands never took the opportunity.

INTRAMURALS

It didn't take me long to figure out that I was not going to make a living being a professional athlete. Not that I had any grand designs about being one; just one season of college basketball and one season of college baseball reinforced my natural predisposition. That, plus the fact that I could play intramurals in college, average 28 points a game, drink a few beers afterwards, and have a lot more fun.

Where my game was at, or better yet, where it wasn't, made playing in college too much like work. Being in college, I was still trying to avoid anything that resembled work.

I settled into a typical college life. The usual mix of classes, roommates, friends, activities, and even colleges. But a constant through my five-year undergraduate progression was sports, and officiating.

In 1975, I stayed in Sterling for my freshman year of college to pursue my athletic career at Sterling College with what little basketball scholarship I received. We now know how that turned out. Near the end of that first year, a buddy of mine was looking into going to the University of Kansas in Lawrence and was openly recruiting a roommate. I originally put him off, but when the basketball team held its post-season meeting in which the coach passed out his off-season conditioning program, I went looking for him and off to Lawrence we went.

We made our way through the usual growing pains of a new school and a new town. We hooked ourselves up with some other guys in our dorm as we tried to put an intramural team together for the array of sports available. In doing so, I found out through the department's bulletin board that they actually paid for officials. It didn't take me long to figure out who I needed to see.

As it turned out, the guy in charge of intramural officials was also the Jayhawk women's softball coach. So we connected immediately, especially after he knew of my background with softball and ASA at the time.

We didn't have to be registered or anything to officiate intramural games, but we went through an orientation process before each season began for each sport. I had enough common knowledge about the sports I was interested in (football, basketball, and softball) that I found out I could survive pretty well. That and the fact that I was willing to work just about any level sent me to the top of the list.

It wasn't unusual for me to play in one game, turn around, and officiate the next, or to work the Independent or Fraternity A leagues on a regular basis. In the year and a half I spend at KU, I worked the Hill Championship (the game between the Fraternity champion and the Independent champion) in football, basketball, and softball. A year and a half after going to Lawrence though, my father passed away and I returned to Sterling.

Over the next two and a half years, while I finished college, I worked some intramural basketball at Sterling College, being the only sport at the school needing officials. I also continued to work softball in the summer at this time.

By the time my final year of school came around, I was going down to the high school to work their intramural games, gratis, if there were no games on campus that night. I also traveled with the college varsity teams as I kept stats and covered games for the school paper, so I got to see a lot of officials work and got to know some of them pretty well. In fact, during the baseball season, most of the officials we had I worked with at one time or another on the softball diamond.

I came within about 60 seconds of getting to step out onto the court for a sub-varsity basketball game in college when it looked like one of the officials wasn't going to show up. As it happened, Sterling's opponent that night was a conference school where my former high school coach was now coaching. As I was about to finish changing, the other official showed and I was sent back to the sidelines.

Knowing what I know now, I would not suggest that someone get into officiating by working intramurals without going through the process of becoming registered and trained by the local association which handles those things. What that opportunity did for me was put me out in the action on more nights than I can remember and allow me to work and develop a style that would become my own, some of which I still use today.

Of course, things are very different now. Nevertheless, during the entire time while I was in college, I cannot remember one person coming up to me to discuss mechanics, rules, situations, or anything that I did out on the field or court. That is where I missed on the technical aspects that is so much a part of how officials are developed today.

It was strictly "on the job training", but it was the best training an official could receive at the time. This was a time before clinics were what they are today and there were few, if any, videos to watch. It was definitely trial and error. With a lot of errors. But those three or four years of working games and handling situations and learning a lot about myself and where I thought my officiating could go, even though I didn't know at the time exactly where I wanted it to go, was a great primer for what was to come.

I GET
REGISTERED

It was during my final year of college when I first became registered in Kansas to work high school basketball. Now I am not familiar with what the process consists of in most other states, but in Kansas, all that being registered meant was that I had paid the appropriate dues and the registering body sent me the appropriate materials.

During the few years up to that point, I had talked with several officials about what the process was to become registered to officiate high school basketball. I also inquired about the process of getting games. Again, during this time, the process was not as technical as it is today with the camps and clinics and the opportunities to be seen.

The process at that time included being available and being in the right place at the right time. But, like today, once an official got there, wherever there was, it was up to the official to prove he or she could stay there.

I'm not sure if it was just that I didn't know, or was content working the intramural contests that were available to me, as to why I hadn't really pursued the registration process before. It wasn't that I didn't know what the process meant as far as getting games, having gone through a similar process years before with ASA.

The event that really pushed me in the direction to eventually becoming registered happened early during that final year of school. Sterling College athletic director and baseball coach at the time, Clair Gleason, called me and fellow student Bill Snyder into his office after a class one day to tell us that the junior high in Lyons was looking for a couple of officials for a basketball game. Evidently, Coach Gleason had already guaranteed our appearance.

He provided each of us with a shirt, whistle, and lanyard, told us to wear black pants, and he let us know what time the game started. He even offered black shoes, except none of them would fit us. I was wearing a size 15 by that time. So we opted for our regular sneakers.

Little about that game has stayed with me. I couldn't tell you who won or lost, or who Lyons even played that day. One thing that has stayed with me though is the lanyard that Coach Gleason gave me for that game. I have used the same one for football to this day, some 35-plus years later.

That junior high game in October pushed me to complete a registration for basketball with the Kansas State High School Activities Association. That registration included required attendance at a rules meeting before the season began, an open-book test to be completed before the season started, and a series of area meetings during the season for things that come up, and were required if an official wanted to be considered for post-season play.

For my part, the area meetings were not required, post-season play was not on my bucket list just yet, but I went to them anyway. I already knew several officials, I was interested in building a schedule, and I was interested in officiating.

In that first year I did build a schedule, small as it was. Consisting of sub-varsity games, junior high games, and freshman games, mostly in Sterling, but a couple of games in Lyons, 8 miles up the road. Besides, a couple of JV games at that time were paying about $40. Man, that was a long way from $4. In addition, this process began to put me in the right place at the right time.

MY PHONE RINGS

My first year as a registered high school basketball official came and went without too many difficulties or bad experiences. I was familiar with most of the schools on my schedule, and even many of the coaches. Some were coaches that were coaching when I played in high school, and some would even be allies of mine, as my officiating advanced. Imagine that.

That first year was the 1979-80 basketball season. In that part of the state, officials mostly worked with regular partners during the year. League commissioners assigned all varsity games for officials and got two officials to work together. Getting a varsity basketball schedule as a new official during this time was difficult, especially if you were a new official working by yourself. If you couldn't get hooked up and partner with another official your only other real option was to find a group of officials into which you could rotate or make yourself available as a fill-in on various occasions.

This first year, I was content filling my schedule with sub-varsity games and such. Remember, I am still in college, with designs on graduating at the end of the year. I don't have any idea what I am going to do for a real job when I get out of school, much less what my officiating career might become.

By working non-varsity games, which, for the most part, were played right before the varsity games, I got the chance to meet many officials and introduce myself; and many of them were familiar to me from my high school playing days, just five years before.

After the season was over, I went through my options on what I could pursue after graduation. I entertained graduate school at colleges in Kansas, Louisiana, and Colorado, pursuing degrees in sports administration or sports information. As luck would have it, as far as my officiating career was concerned, none of those options materialized.

I odd-jobbed it through the summer of 1980, primarily through a jobs program offered in Kansas for students. It had been my primary job source since my early high school days. It provided me with jobs with city departments, schools, recreation departments, and this particular summer, driving a truck and tractor during wheat harvest. And, of course, I was still umpiring softball all summer long.

It was through this program that I found my first real job, which would become how I made my living immediately after college. My title was Assistant Superintendent of Recreation for the Lyons Recreation Commission. In actuality, the job was not nearly as impressive as the title. But it was a job I was comfortable with. After going through the initial interview process, and getting all the paperwork in order, I wouldn't get started until November. So through the summer, and until I began my job in November, I was still living at home in Sterling.

In the meantime, I registered again over the summer with the high school activities association for basketball, not really knowing what the season might hold in store for me, or what I might be able to provide once the season began. Then, one night while sitting at home in October, the greatest thing happened.

My phone rang. Okay, it was my mom's phone, but the call was for me.

On the other end of the line was a basketball official from Lyons, Curtis Miller. I had seen him at the area meetings and he and his partner the previous year had worked some varsity games after my sub-varsity games.

Curtis was looking for a new partner and he wanted to know if I would be interested. He didn't know that I would be moving to Lyons in about a month starting a new job, which would now turn out to be beneficial. He remembered seeing me referee the previous year. His partner was leaving Lyons, and Kansas, due to a job transfer, so Curtis needed someone to work his upcoming schedule with him. Looking back on it now, Curtis was probably running out of names by the time he came upon mine.

I was as familiar with Curtis, as I was with just about every official in the area, though I didn't really know him. Nor did I know what kind of a schedule I was taking on. Regardless, it didn't take me long to say yes.

As it turned out, Curtis, along with his father, Cecil, were farmers outside of Lyons, with a big operation, centered mostly on wheat and corn. In fact, I had often driven by some great looking fields of corn along the highway between Sterling and Lyons. Those fields belonged to Curtis and his dad. Curtis wound up being a great first partner for me. He had a great sense of humor, not taking himself too seriously, and he got along very well with the coaches, most of whom knew him well.

As for that first varsity schedule, looking back, there was nothing spectacular about it then, or now. That first schedule included 12 varsity games: Chase @ Little River; Marquette @ Hutchinson-Trinity; Lucas-Luray @ Sylvan Grove; Chase @ Marquette; Dorrance @ Gorham; Garden Plain @ Norwich; St John @ Macksville; Canton-Galva @ Little River; Ellinwood @ Stafford; Kinsley @ Stafford; Nashville-Zenda @ Norwich; Larned @ Hoisington. Along with these games were about six junior high games in Lyons and Sterling. My first varsity check was for $37.20, $30 for the game and $7.20 mileage. Yes, I still have a copy of that first varsity schedule. In fact, I have every varsity basketball schedule I have ever worked since.

Those from Kansas will recognize most of those schools. Some, like Marquette, Dorrance, Gorham, and Nashville-Zenda, may not be as recognizable. That is because they, like many others, have since closed. Most of the rest are not that much bigger now than they were then. I finished the year with two post-season Class 1A regional games at Little River.

After the season, Curtis informed me that he was giving up basketball. I don't think it was anything I did, or anything that happened to us during the year. He had two young boys at home, he and his wife also took on foster kids, and farming was taking a lot of his time.

So I took over his schedule beginning the next season. Basketball would become my number one sport to officiate. I was now off and running. Though it would be a while before I could feel like I was really running in the right direction.

DONE WITH ASA

I am not sure it was any one thing, but a series of events and opportunities finally led to my conclusion. I was finished with the Amateur Softball Association (ASA).

Even though for nearly 10 years it had been my bread and butter; even though ASA had really given me the first opportunity to develop as an official; even though I had put myself in a position to work many post-season state and regional tournaments at the end of those summers; and even though nothing else in my officiating resume at the time would completely fill that void.

The powder blue of the Elbeco shirt was my only real connection with officiating until I became registered to officiate high school basketball in 1979. But by that time, something changed. Actually, many things changed.

I would like to think that all officials strive to become better each time they step out onto the floor or onto the field. I am not naïve enough to think that is true in all cases for all officials, but it was for me then and still is today.

And when an official strives to become better, and does actually become better, that official receives some recognition through better regular season assignments and post-season assignments. That began to change for me with ASA.

I worked my first state tournament in Kansas for ASA in 1976, when I was 18 years old, the girls 15-and-under fast-pitch tournament, held in Manhattan. I had been working fast-pitch softball for four years and this was my first real exposure to post-season play. The state commissioner, Jerry Stremel, who lived in Hutchinson, about 20 miles away, called about two weeks before the tournament and asked if I was interested.

Jerry was old school ASA before old school. Jerry operated the ASA state office out of his old milk producers' office in a small building on South Main in Hutchinson, Kansas. Not that being the state commissioner was a full-time job, just that Jerry, being retired, made it one to keep himself busy.

From that first state tournament on, I worked a state tournament in one class or another each year I was registered with ASA. The next year I was selected to work the women's major state tournament, held annually in Kingman at that time. That was also the summer before my first year at the University of Kansas. That year the men's tournament was held in Topeka, after I had already moved to Lawrence to begin school at KU. That opened some doors for me with the softball community in Topeka, the center of fast-pitch softball in Kansas at the time.

I returned to Kingman for the women's tournament the following year. But before I left to return to Lawrence, I got a call to fill in at the men's tournament early in the week when a couple of local umpires had to drop out. I worked two games a night on Tuesday, Wednesday, and Thursday of that first men's tournament. In fact, my first game of the tournament was on the plate for Margie's Café out of Wichita. The same Margie's mentioned earlier during that 1980 near death experience, and at this time, the defending state champion.

For the next few years, I picked up two state tournaments each year. Partially, I would like to think due to my ability, but also, I know, due to my location to the tournament sites, which meant that they wouldn't have to pick up a hotel tab to have me around for three or four days.

But around 1982 that all changed. After an AIAW softball regional in the spring of 1981 at Kansas University, (the AIAW was a precursor to the NCAA taking over women's athletics) and a men's fast-pitch regional in St Joseph, Missouri, that same year over Labor Day weekend, the ASA never seemed to be the same.

Kansas ASA came out and stated that an umpire could only work one major state tournament in a year. And the ASA nationally came out with a set of standard mechanics that all umpires, who were to be considered for post-season play, were to adhere to. A standard that Kansas adopted as well.

This, plus a new hierarchy in the state, just didn't seem to jibe with my philosophy at the time. Because my interest now

33

also included basketball, I began watching a lot of it on television, including the NBA. And there were many old school officials still working in the NBA, Mendy Rudolph, Earl Strom, Jack Madden, Ritchie Powers and so on. Trust me, those guys were not using standard mechanics. Neither were the baseball umpires I saw on Saturday afternoons.

I was selected to work the men's state fast-pitch tournament again in Topeka in 1982. I knew before I was even selected that this was going to be my last summer with ASA. Knowing the direction that ASA was taking, I was ready to move on. But I had not told this to anyone else yet, and wouldn't until the next spring came around.

Another factor was that slow pitch softball was getting bigger. I was seeing this through my job with the recreation commission and in Hutchinson, which was setting up as a power in Kansas for a new softball organization USSSA (United States Slo-Pitch Softball Association). It was stepping up and challenging ASA with formats and an organization that was player and team friendly, and it offered a variety of classes and post-season options for every skill level. USSSA promoted itself to teams and players, leaving ASA behind.

Working in recreation, we had switched our leagues over to USSSA, since league champions got an automatic berth into the state tournaments of their designated class of play. USSSA also would routinely designate a variety of tournaments throughout the year in which the champions could qualify for state tournament play as well.

I also switched over to baseball full time after that summer and began filling my springs umpiring college baseball and my next few summers with playing slow pitch softball.

I really never returned to ASA as an umpire, and I don't think my defection made any real dent in their existence. ASA is still alive and doing well today as USA Softball. In fact, after several years of decline, it is making a comeback of sorts. I even volunteered to help at a couple of ASA national tournaments in Topeka during the early 2000's.

It's been over 20 years since I have been really active with the organization. But those years of softball provided a lot of great memories. A lot of great friends. A lot of great times.

GETTING A
SCHEDULE

Obviously, getting my first schedule was not difficult. Curtis Miller already had that lined up when I joined him for that first year. But now, with Curtis gone, I was left with not only the task of putting together a schedule, but also finding someone to work with me.

My options were limited at best. As I mentioned before, most basketball referees at this time were working with established partners. Since I was not willing to work as a fill-in, I needed to find someone to work with me.

I did have a few choices. That first year, I actually opted for two officials. Both were currently employed at Sterling College, one was an admission counselor who had a decent background in basketball and had been working some, while the other was actually the head football coach, who I would later find out, was actually on his way out.

The down and dirty part of actually getting my schedule was left to calling the commissioners of the area leagues and letting them know what was going on; hopeful they would understand and be willing to put a second-year varsity official out on the floor in charge with a couple of marginal, but capable, partners. One of these commissioners was responsible for three leagues, one of small schools, another of schools slightly larger, and a third league that consisted of the larger schools in the area, though it only had six schools total. A few other commissioners, with leagues consisting of smaller schools, were willing to provide games, not that I had much negotiating power at this time.

As it turned out, being a little more aggressive than Curtis, I was able to fill most of the Tuesday/Friday play dates much easier than I was expecting; partly because I was willing to work anywhere at any time.

Basically, for the next several years, that is the way each season went. Over those years, I worked with four different partners for the most part, the two I mentioned earlier, a third who I considered to be in the same category, though he had several years of experience, but could never really advance much, and a fourth who even during this time was very long in the tooth, but continued to work even long after he and I parted ways.

I made it a policy then (and now) that I would fill my schedule with games on a first-come, first-served basis. Yes, I did want the better games and the better leagues, but I also did not want to completely fill my schedule with just a couple of leagues. First, I did not want to alienate any commissioner or burn any bridges, and second, I believe that leads to a situation that I refer to as "wearing out one's welcome". A situation where you see the same teams, coaches and players time and time again. The reality is nothing good is going to come from this kind of situation. So, I have always felt that it is best to see a larger variety of teams, rather than the same teams over and over.

Ideally, I did not want any more than three games in any one particular league, and with about seven leagues within an hour's drive, that was a doable situation. By doing that, I was able to work everything from schools classified as 1A (enrollments of less than 100) to the largest, class 6A (enrollments of as many as 1,000 or more) But, if you were going to work in that part of the state, that was what you had to be prepared to do.

And really, it was fine. The large classes played a different game, but I looked forward to each night regardless of where I went. As time went on, and I became more familiar with the schools and the leagues, and they with me, I began to develop some familiarity and a comfort level that allowed me to look forward to going back to some schools each year.

But during this time, working and trying to maintain a schedule, there was the effort and, sometimes, frustration, of bringing my partners along. My partners were older, maybe not that much more experienced overall, but, generally, not at the level I saw myself going to at the time.

Part of it was a difference in officiating philosophy, part of it was a difference in looking the part, and part of it was a difference in raw ability. This is not an ego trip or conceit, but I knew I was better and I was ready, willing, and able to put my whistle where my stripes were, so to speak. One of my partners could never understand why he was not getting the number or quality post-season assignments that I or other officials were getting at the time. Even in the mid-1980's he had a hard time separating the black and white of the rule book from the grey on the floor.

Part of my assurance in my ability came from the fact that I received post-season games every year. In Kansas, that consisted of one week of regional play for 1A schools, and a week of sub-state play for all schools, prior to the state tournament. And in each of those years, my post-season took a step forward. After that first year of first round regional games, the next two seasons saw "full" 1A regionals and first-round sub-state games in a couple of the middle classifications.

Another reason I knew that I was headed in the right direction was the fact that I was receiving more recommendations from schools during the year than those of my partners, which was (and still is) the basic criteria for getting post-season games. For me, it all boiled down to a few simple issues: mechanics, presence, and the ability to handle situations. Those were things that my partners at the time lacked and were never really able to fully embrace.

But that would soon change.

I GOT A 6A

Post-season games were my carrot, and, for the most part, continued to be so through my career. We all knew the mechanics of getting post-season games at the time, the format that they were assigned and the timetable. The state high school activities association in Kansas makes all post-season assignments. Actually, it's just one person.

It was not a job I envied. It takes a lot of work filling post-season games in a multitude of locations, classes, and situations. Then take into account situations involving officials, travel, possible match-ups, who has recommended who, and the whole experience involves burning a lot of midnight oil.

We all knew that two weeks prior to each round of post-season play, we could expect assignments in our mailbox on Friday of that week. We all knew the assigner from the association and his timetable. And each year it rarely varied. We knew what the envelope looked like. We knew what paperwork looked like and what to expect in those envelopes.

The timetable was such that pairings were not completed, but we knew which teams were grouped together. So part of the anticipation was trying to figure out the regional or sub-state where we thought each of us would go. Since teams were to only recommend officials who had worked their games or they had seen work somewhere that allowed us to try and out-guess the assigner. Sometimes we were right on. Other times, assignments seemed like they came right out of the blue.

Of course some of it also hinged on availability of officials. That availability, or lack of, could throw a curve at the whole situation.

Though the schedule has changed, as has the assigner, I still get antsy when I know that post-season assignments are coming out. As my wife can attest, I have always enjoyed mail, but the anticipation of post-season assignments from the association only served to heighten that sense. Then during this time, add to it the still naïve, youthful, anticipation that came with each post-season, and you get someone who knew what time his mail arrived and arranged to go by the house while the envelopes were still warm from the postman's bag.

Once the envelopes arrive, the process involves sorting through the details of the assignment. This includes the location of the tournament, the potential sites of first-round match-ups, who your partner, and potential partners will be, the tournament director, who gets to drive and receive that all-important mileage check, and completing the paperwork that must be returned to the association to confirm acceptance of the assignment.

Of course, by confirming the assignment that also means there is a process to follow when an assignment must be turned away. Thankfully, I have only had to do that once in nearly 40 years.

That occasion was a first-round assignment of a sub-state being hosted by my then hometown of Lyons. The circumstances surrounding that involved me having taken a week of vacation just a few weeks prior for a cruise, and my boss at the time taking his vacation the same week as the sub-state. So in our small one-man shop of a recreation department, that left me to cover evening events and opening and closing facilities. As a result, there would be no basketball for me that week.

It didn't turn out to hurt me in the long run, though at the time, not truly aware of the entire process, I was pretty fearful about having to contact the activities association and the assistant director at the time to tell him I was turning it back. For me, he was the all-mighty, and I was just some wet-behind-the-ear basketball official who could end up being a grease spot on the highway to the next game, if he wanted.

That episode aside, post-season assignments varied for me. Most were not very far away, and most, at this time, involved working with a lot of the more experienced and capable officials of the time, a development I always looked forward to. These were some of the guys who I knew were working a lot of the better games, and I still needed to prove to others I was in that category and, very capable.

By receiving these assignments some two weeks prior to the games, that meant spending the final weeks of the season checking scores in the newspaper, conferring with other officials about their assignments and potential games, and anticipating (sometimes bracing for) whatever games lay ahead.

In any case, it was, and still is, one of the most exciting times of the season for me; not only the expectation of working games with great intensity, but the hope and anticipation of where I might actually end up.

That included such noteworthy locations as Sylvan Grove, Lincoln, Moundridge, Goessel, Pratt-Skyline, and my hometown Sterling. So this time, in 1984, when I received my envelope in the mail, I was a little more hopeful for something like Pratt, Larned, Ellsworth, or maybe even Buhler. Trust me when I say that I was not even remotely expecting to read what was stretched across the top of the first page:

TO: Class 6A Sub-State Basketball Officials

SITE: Dodge City Civic Center

HOST: Dodge City High School

You have been selected to officiate in the Class 6A Sub-State Basketball Boys/Girls Tournament listed above. To accept this assignment, please complete the form enclosed and return it to the KSHSAA office immediately. If you cannot accept this assignment, please contact our office immediately at . . .

You would have thought I won the Powerball Lottery. I guess, as far as I was concerned, it was the lottery.

I have no idea how this came to be. Anything would be speculation on my part. But I did have the Hutchinson High School girls during the season, twice actually. And I know that when the post-season assignments are made, there is consideration made to the teams playing and the officials they have recommended. Plus the fact that with Dodge City as the host, that would mean there would be an effort to include someone that Hutchinson would be familiar with, since they would be some two hours from home. The other schools in the four-team sub-state included Great Bend and Garden City.

In those days, an official worked one girl's semi-final on Thursday and one boy's semi-final on Friday. Then each official would work one of the finals on Saturday night. Another official from Lyons and I traveled together for the tournament, working with two officials from Pratt. Each night meant working with a different partner, with the two of us from Lyons working the girl's final together on Saturday.

I don't recall anything especially important about that tournament now, except for one thing. Thinking back now that one thing may have been the most important thing I did all weekend, as we will see later. I wound up calling a technical foul on a player for the Dodge City boys. After the game the AD walked us back to the locker room and inquired about what the kid did, not to question my reasoning for calling the T, but to see if there was anything else that the school needed to address with the situation.

I informed him that everything was fine; it was just a situation that needed attention right then and there was no further incident after that. The rest of the weekend went well. After it was over, I really didn't feel any different for having worked that sub-state over any other post-season tournament I had worked before. I guess, in reality that confirmed my feelings that I belonged all along.

They would not be the last 6A post-season games I would work, nor the last time I worked in Dodge City.

PART-TIME, FULL-TIME

The top of the mountain for any high school basketball official is a state tournament. State tournaments come in a variety of forms all over the country. Some operate boys and girls tournaments separately, due to times of the year that seasons are played, the format for qualifying, and the fact that in some states, because they operate under different associations.

In Kansas, state tournaments are combined into single sites for the same class, since they operate in the same season, under the same rules, and are officiated by the same officials. That process didn't come easy, and was not always done that way. Now the six classes of competition each complete their own boys and girls state tournaments at a site specific to each class.

In 1987, that format involved eight boys and eight girls teams advancing to the state tournament in each class. Tournaments began on Thursday with quarter-final games for both boys and girls. That meant that eight games were played on that first day, four boys and four girls. Even under the best of circumstances, one would not expect all eight games to be completed in one day at one site. And they weren't.

Boy's games were played at what was considered the primary site, or the site for the semi-finals and finals. Girl's games, on the other hand, were contested at a secondary site close to the primary site on the same day and at the same time. Then all semi-finals were played on Friday, with third-place games and championship games played on Saturday.

During this time, post-season games were officiated by two officials. With a single tournament, you could have eight officials, each working one game each day. But now, with a full set of games being played on that first day in two different locations, there had to be some way to make sure those games were officiated by qualified officials. Thus, came the format that officials at the time understood as "Part-Time, Full-Time".

Part-Time officials were selected to officiate one game on that first day of quarterfinal games. It might be a boy's game; it might be a girl's game. Full-time officials were selected to officiate not only one game on the quarterfinal day, but also one game during the semi-finals on Friday, and either a third-place or championship game on Saturday. That meant there were eight full-time officials and eight part-time officials at each tournament site.

What the activities association did was select the top 48 recommended officials as full-time officials for the six tournaments; then the next 48 recommended officials comprised those that made up the part-time crews. In assignments for the quarter-final games, the association matched up each full-time official with a part-time official. So in each of the six tournaments, there were eight officials who would officiate one game, and eight officials who would officiate three games.

Obviously, any official getting this far wanted to work full-time. That was a great way to cap off the season, officiating three games in a state tournament. But, if you were like I was at that time, working a state tournament as a part-time official certainly wasn't the worst way to finish your season.

The notification for the state tournament followed the same timetable as the other post-season games. Notification came out on the Friday, two weeks prior to the tournament. Or, the Friday of regional play for Class 1A and the final Friday of regular season play for all other classifications.

This season was no different than those preceding it. My schedule was getting better; it was full, and I had been getting to know many of the coaches and schools in the area, now going on my seventh year of varsity basketball games, and my eighth year overall.

By this time, I had also settled in to work with a couple of guys near my own age. We had a similar philosophy about officiating, but each of us brought our own personal perspective, style, and abilities to the game. We had all grown up playing the game, and we used that knowledge to help with our understanding of what it looked like from behind the whistle.

By now, I had also become Director of Recreation for the Lyons Recreation Commission. This had afforded me the opportunity to work on my officiating career by providing me with more flexibility and an avenue to work with other officials in other sports and venues. It also didn't hurt that a couple of my board members were these same two officials who I was spending most of my Tuesday and Friday nights with.

In fact this last Friday night of the regular season, I was finishing up with a game in Hutchinson. The same Hutchinson that I am sure helped me get that 6A sub-state a few years before. Only this time I was meeting my partner at the game, since I would be coming back from our annual state park and recreation conference and would not have time to make it back to Lyons in time to meet up with him before he left.

I had been out of town for a couple of days and obviously had no access to my mail or any information about the upcoming post-season. However, my partner on this final regular season night did, through his wife who worked for the post office part-time. And he knew that I was out of town and was meeting him at the game site. So when he walked into the locker room at the arena, I had no idea what was about to hit me.

He wondered if I had anyone at home checking my mail, and, in fact how long I had actually been gone. I reminded him that I had not been home and was on my way back from the conference. (Of which he was fully aware. Remember, he was one of my board members I answered to.) With that, he smiled and informed me that he had someone check my mail before he left to come to the game and handed me an envelope from the activities association. (I don't think the federal authorities would look kindly on this today, but in small town Kansas in the 1980's, people knew how to make things happen.) I recognized the envelope. It looked like so many others I had received. The only difference this time was that it came at a time that I would not normally receive such a piece of mail.

Now we had all talked about working a state tournament. All of us were anticipating the day that we would eventually receive one. We all believed we would, it was just a matter of when. For me and my partner that night, it had arrived.

Sitting in that locker room, it was the same feeling I had with that 6A sub-state tournament just a few years before. Only this time it was better. I was going to work a state tournament. As it turned out, it was the Class 3A tournament, which was in Hutchinson every year. And my partner that night was also working in the tournament as well, also his first.

The difference was his assignment was as a full-time official, which meant three games, while mine was only as a part-time official, and just one game. But that first step was taken.

That first game for me was a girls contest at the secondary site between Pleasant Ridge and Erie. My partner was a football coach from a school just south of Hutchinson and a veteran official of many years. And regardless of how well we conducted our pregame, he was going to work his game, his way, with his habits coming through. Me, I was just going to try and stay out of the way. I didn't know either team. I was just glad to get the game started . . . and know that I hadn't forgotten any part of my uniform.

I had a tape made, but-just my luck-I had it made in Beta format. For those of you who may not know, Beta has gone the way of cassette tapes and vinyl records. I still have that old Beta tape. I guess I should see about getting it converted to something more useful. Then again, maybe I will find out that I was not as good as I had hoped.

But beside my name the next year in the official's directory would be a capital "S" designating a state basketball tournament on my listing. Only 96 names in the book would have that designation. As chance would have it, that was the final year for part-time officials. The next season, the activities association reworked the state tournament format and did away with the secondary site, moving the girls' quarter-final contests to the primary site with a Wednesday start. That meant that those who were previously part-time officials were going to work two games; one Wednesday and one Thursday, while the former full-time officials would also now work just two games, one semi-final on Friday and a third-place or championship game on Saturday.

That next season, I was ready for the mail. Lo and behold, another envelope arrived. This time, Class 1A at Hays for Wednesday and Thursday. In addition, one official was appointed to handle a pre-tournament meeting with all officials on that first day. Next to my name was an asterisk indicating that it was I who was to lead that meeting in Hays on Wednesday.

As an added "bonus", the association sent one of its directors to each tournament site each day to oversee the proceedings and take care of any administrative issues. On that first day, they also sat in on the pre-tournament officials meeting. That day, the director on hand wasn't just one of the assistants, but THE Executive Director, Nelson Hartman himself. It was bad enough that I was the "pup" in the room, now I had Mr. Hartman looking over my shoulder and listening to every word I had to say. I can't help but think that I was set-up. Not necessarily to fail, but to find out just what this kid from central Kansas could really do.

My partner for one of my games that year was a "veteran" official from western Kansas who had been officiating longer than I had been alive. Let's just say that what "Sonny" lacked in mechanics, he made up for in experience. Twenty years later, "Sonny" was still registered and working in the western Kansas. My guess is that his mechanics hadn't changed a lot.

MY PHONE RINGS
(AGAIN)

By now you have the idea that my basketball officiating career had become fairly well established. Through 10 years I had worked post-season games in nine of those years, or each year that I had a varsity schedule. Everything from 1A regional games to sub-state games in nearly every other classification, to three state tournament assignments.

So as I complete my 10th year, I turn my attention to putting together my schedule for my 11th year. I am still pretty much working with the same bunch of guys. We switch back and forth between each other going to our usual stops throughout the area.

But one morning after this particular season I am sitting around the house getting ready to leave for work, when, just like nine years earlier, the phone rings. This time, though, it is my phone as I am now married and on my own. But short of some work related calamity, my phone hardly ever rang this time of day.

When I answer, a hear a deep voice on the other end that introduces himself as J.C. Riekenberg, Athletic Director at Dodge City High School. The voice, I was not that familiar with, but I knew that name. If you knew anything about high school sports in western Kansas, you knew who J.C. was.

I'm sure he heard my slobbering over the phone even though I had no idea why he was calling me. I soon found out. He cut right to the chase. He explained to me that they had a basketball tournament in Dodge City in January called the Tournament of Champions and he wanted to know if I was interested in working.

If you have any doubt about my answer, trust me when I say I said yes. But in my mind I'm thinking, "Are you out of your mind? Of course I'm interested. This is just the biggest mid-season high school basketball tournament in the state of Kansas. Are you nuts?"

He said he would also like for me to come out and work a couple of regular season games as well, especially before the tournament in mid-January. "Sure." He worked around my filled dates and we found a couple of dates that fit everyone's schedule.

I don't know of a time before mid-season basketball tournaments during the high school season in Kansas. As a kid and until my freshman year in high school in 1971, I knew of mid-season tournaments. Sterling always went to the Mid-Winter Classic in St John. That is until Sterling started its own tournament my sophomore year.

These tournament weeks during the season, are determined by the activities association when they can be held. Typically they fall during the last two weeks of January. During my high school years, this also meant that they were typically boys' tournaments as the girls were just getting the opportunity to actually play basketball then.

For the most part, these are eight-team formats with a consolation bracket and winner's bracket. Each team gets three games over a three-day span. In some cases, as was the case with my hometown tourney, those three days could be spread over the entire week. Two first-round games were played on Monday, with the other two first-round games played on Tuesday. Monday's losers would play an early game on Tuesday before the second set of first-round games.

Thursday would be the semi-finals, with the Tuesday losers in action before these games; followed by final action on Friday night with a full set of four games to finish out the tournament.

But most tournaments followed the format of everyone playing on Thursday, with losers and winners paired off and coming back on Friday, with final match-ups on Saturday. This was true of the Tournament of Champions or the "TOC" as it is known. There are several tournaments across the state during this time of year. Some of the top tournaments include the Four-State Classic in Coffeyville, the Orange and Black Classic in Colby and the McPherson Invitational. But the TOC, in my biased opinion, is the best.

The TOC began its run in 1944, just as the name indicates. It brought the state champions together from the previous year, with other top teams from the area. As Dodge City's athletic director, J.C. was the tournament director and in charge. A fact that anyone who knew anything about the tourney knew all too well. J.C. didn't start the tourney, but he had done his duty to carry on its well-known tradition. So when he called he really didn't need to explain the Tournament of Champions, where it was, or when it was. I already knew.

J.C. had been the school's football coach for some time, and a good one. He stepped down from coaching in the 1970's to start his reign as the A.D. To say that J.C. was a no-nonsense kind of guy is like saying Michael Jordan was a basketball player. There was not much gray area with J.C. If he said jump, most everyone wanted to know how high.

By the time I became involved with the TOC it consisted of a core of four or five teams that alternated trips to Dodge City every other year, with a couple of teams that committed to the tourney a few years prior. Add the host team Dodge City and then a small school, typically from western Kansas, which gets its opportunity to take on the big boys.

Also, by the time I made my first trip to Dodge City they were using three officials for each game, something that was not done across the entire state, including post-season play. This year, the officiating crew consisted of myself, and four very well-seasoned partners, who I knew, including one official who was not only a hunting buddy of J.C.'s, but also a Division I college basketball official. They included Don Ward, John Hamm, Stu Chance, and J.C.'s hunting buddy, Paul Shelite.

That first year, I pretty much just did what they said. Other than Dodge City, I had no personal knowledge of any of the other teams. But I knew of most of them. There was Wichita East and Wichita Heights, probably the two top teams at that time in the city of Wichita. Both had deep reputations and this year, they had the two best players in the state in

Cortez Barnes of Heights and Mark Hutton from East. In fact, they wound up in the finals, going to double overtime.

Atchison was there with head coach Chic Downing. Chic was a black head coach for a predominately black basketball team and he didn't put up with anything from his players. He was also one of the state's top softball players. Chic was about 6'7" with the wingspan of a 7-footer.

We each worked two games a day, with two of us working three games due to the fact that five of us were working the entire tournament. It would be a few years after my arrival before we added a sixth official, which then meant that everyone would work just two games each day, one in the afternoon and one in the evening.

The atmosphere around the Tournament of Champions was, and is, completely different than any other basketball I have experienced. State tournaments included. The play was different, the attitude was different. Even our shirts were different.

I don't know when it all started; all I know is that I had to wedge my double-X body into a regular large shirt that had seen more than just a few tournaments. J.C. finally relented and purchased new shirts for us the next year that we put to use for several years after. For the TOC, I put on four different-styled referee shirts. Not black and white striped, mind you, but shirts that would more closely remind you of softball jerseys or bowling or golf shirts.

J.C. also took care of any fringe details. All we needed to do was referee basketball. Oh, there was a tournament committee, but J.C. was the tournament director, PR director, and head bouncer. It was his way or the highway. Only 12 players could suit up for each team. Thirty band members? Sorry only 25 get in free. Cheerleaders must wear numbers assigned to them so they can be judged. They don't want to wear their numbers? Nice seeing you, have a safe trip home. Want a seat for the finals Saturday night? Tickets are for sale at the ticket office.

This went on for 25 years for me, through two relocations, several other tournament partners, and even two facilities. The TOC was still the highlight of my basketball season. J.C. eventually retired altogether. Before he left, I told myself that I would see how things went in deciding how long I would keep going back. Like that pink bunny, I kept going and going and going. When I finished, in 2014, Stu and I were still there, but other referees had changed, though the majority of us were in place year after year.

It was a great three days. My wife and I were like family in Dodge City during this time. We were treated great, the hospitality room was great, and the crowds were great. It was as much fun as I had doing anything all year. For me, the TOC was like a second beginning to the basketball season. From this point on, each year, the basketball season began to get very serious.

Thanks J.C. Though thank you will never be enough.

Dodge City TOC Officials (2009): L-R: Kevin Heft, Josh Nelson, Stu Chance, myself, Todd Tichenor, John Mies.

MY LAST
DOUBLE-DIP

I was young. A lot younger than I am now.

When you are young you do a lot of things that you wouldn't even think of doing when you get older. But when you are young you are bulletproof. What happened to someone else could never happen to you. How could (enter a name here) let something like that happen to him or her? What were they thinking? That they was some kind of Superman?

But you know, there isn't a basketball official around, or any sports official for that matter, that hasn't done something to test that theory. And some continue to test it, even when they know it means not giving their best effort. Here is how it all came about for me.

This was my ninth year of basketball and my schedule was pretty full of high school games, and college games as well. Like most young basketball officials who are worth their salt, I tried to advance to the next level. By the time I began to work state high school tournaments, I also began getting some college games.

At first it was college women, but my heart was set on moving to the men's game. But during this year, the 1988-89 season, with a full high school schedule, I had about 12 college women's games, as well as the opportunity to work the NJCAA Women's Region 6 tournament at the end of the year.

The college games gave me the chance to work some games in November that were spread out enough to allow me to get some rhythm and feel for a basketball game before the regular season got hectic. By the time December, and the high school games came along, for an official working both high school and college games, it would not be anything to be on the floor four or five nights each week.

By December 9th of this season, I had nine official games under my belt and probably three or four controlled scrimmages out of the way. It has always been my practice in accepting ballgames in any sport, that when I get a game, I keep a game. So, when I got my high school schedule for this season,

I was scheduled for a game at Russell High school against Hays High School on December 9, which I knew at the time with the schools being only about 20 miles apart, would be a rivalry game.

At some point during that summer, I picked up my college games for the upcoming season. When the dates come out, one date I received was December 9. Being a junior college game, I knew that if I got a women's game on this day, it would be in, what many schools did early in the season, a tournament format. In other words, it would be four teams matched up against each other, with two of them switching opponents between the first and second days. I also knew that most of these tournaments included both men's and women's games.

That being the case, women's games were typically played at 2 pm and 6 pm with men's games at 4 pm and 8 pm. Knowing where I would actually be going would not come out until sometime around October, so I decided to hold out until I was sure of my game assignment that day before jumping to any conclusions about what I would ultimately need to do.

When October comes and the college officials get together for their annual pre-season clinic, schedules are handed out to everyone. This involved everyone checking dates for game sites, times, and all of the previously determined game dates handed out previously by the assigning commissioner. Basically just making sure everything matches up to what we agreed to some months ago.

When I get my schedule, the first thing I check is December 9. Well, what do you know? I am scheduled for a 2 pm game at Barton County Community College in Great Bend. For those of you who know little about Kansas geography, Great Bend is basically about 30 miles from Russell, and on the way. That means I can finish my college game in Great Bend, shower, drive to Russell and still get there in plenty of time to make the 6 pm start for my girls/boys high school doubleheader.

My partner for my college game was a guy that is coming from another direction, so I plan to meet him at the game site. My partner for the high school doubleheader was one of my regular partners from Lyons, who was also an alumni of Barton County, so he decided to ride along with me to Great Bend, then we would go on to Russell from there.

My college game goes smoothly. Or as smoothly as any early-season college women's game is going to go. To begin with it is at 2 pm, which meant the home team would not be playing. That meant it would probably be two teams I would not normally see during the year. It also meant few, if any, fans were in the stands to watch.

I am in no rush to move along quickly after the game. I can take my time to shower, unwind, and maybe even grab a bite to eat before we have to be in Russell by 5-5:15 pm, for a 6 pm start to our girls' game.

We get to Russell in plenty of time. We take our time to dress and prepare for the game. Again, we know that with this being a game between Russell and Hays, even though the two schools were not in the same league, would be fiercely contested. So we preparing ourselves for the things that will most likely present itself when two rivals meet.

The girls' game goes by without a hitch. And really, the boys' game was not something that turned into a donnybrook or anything. Both teams played hard, both coaches coached just as hard, but the games were very workable.

I don't know when exactly it happened, but at some point in the second half of the boys' game, it happened. Somebody put a piano on my back. Or maybe it was that plow that got hooked onto my belt. Or maybe it was someone who put up that wall that I ran into. Whatever it was, wherever it was, whenever it was, it had me.

Remember, this is 1989 and games in this area, including the three I was on, were all pretty much worked with just two officials. And going into the fourth quarter of the boys' game in

Russell I was working on 104 minutes of basketball. Three games in about seven hours.

Between my dogs barking, my calves burning, and me watching the clock, the night was not ending fast enough for me. I literally felt like an old man when the final buzzer sounded. If I looked anything like I felt, I'm surprised someone didn't offer me a wheelchair.

I knew when I sat down in the locker room after those games, this would be the last time I tried to cover multiple assignments in one day. Sure, I would work more than one game a day, but not three and certainly not three games using two-person mechanics. Sure, I would work three games at one site, including a sub-varsity game and two varsity contests using three-person mechanics, with both teams knowledgeable of the circumstances. This was different. This was three quality games that one site didn't know about the other.

The college teams expected my best, thinking their's was the only game I had that day. That I would coast to try and save myself for two games later that night was not on their minds. And when the afternoon started, it was not on mine as well. I wasn't that smart then, and I would like to think that faced with the same situation again, I have too much respect for the game and what I have been entrusted to do.

For the high school teams, their world was all in that gym in Russell that night. The idea that any other game was being played was not on their minds. And not on mine until that approaching moment in the final half of that final game. And they too, expected my best that night. Oh, they got it, just that my best would not be the best I could have offered had my 2 pm appointment not been on my schedule.

But as a result of my efforts on this night, another development presented itself that affected my schedule to the end. Hays High School, the team that Russell played that night, was impressed enough with my partner and I that they called when confirming their officials for the next season and asked if we would be interested in working a couple of games for them, including the return match between Russell and Hays.

Those games, in turn, resulted in the opportunity to work in their early-season tournament, the Hays City Shootout, a boys and girls eight-team tourney during the first week of December. An assignment, like the TOC, that remained a part of my schedule every year.

Despite the rewards that came, I chose not to embark on anything like it again. I found out what my limits were. From that point on, when I filled a date during the basketball season, I made sure that all my filled-date sheets were marked so those dates would not come up in any discussion of possible opportunities. No questions about where games were located, or what time they started, or how far away they were. All of that was of no importance to me anymore.

I am older. A lot older now, and wiser, than I was before.

THE LYONS
CONNECTION

It was mentioned earlier that as I put my basketball officiating schedule together each year, there was a core of officials that would comprise the partners that would make up most of my officiating schedule during those early years. Living in Lyons, this core was primarily officials from Lyons. But it did include, from time to time, officials from some of the other small towns in the immediate area.

My initial football crew did include an official from Great Bend, about 30 miles away. And any baseball I was working was done with umpires from places other than Lyons. But basketball gave me the opportunity to work primarily with other officials from the immediate area.

For a community of just over 3,000 people, Lyons really did have a pretty good number of officials. We always got together before each of the respective seasons to work on the open book test, and we usually had enough officials around to take care of the sub-varsity and junior high games of the schools in the county, of which there were five.

In basketball, again, most of the games were worked by officials who worked together as partners. But that didn't mean they all were. Initially, I did not have a regular partner, so I had to piece-meal my early schedules together with whoever was available. But eventually, we were able to put together a core of officials who were interchangeable on most game nights.

All told, there were about 10 officials from Lyons working varsity basketball. Of those 10, six of us were a core group that would find themselves with any one of the other on any given night. Five of us were fairly young, for the most part. By young I am talking about early 20's to early 30's. The other was in the twilight of his officiating career, having worked about as many years as the rest of us were old.

But not only did we officiate together, we also sought each other out socially as well. I was running the recreation department; two others were on my board of directors, including one who was the business manager at the local hospital and another that ran the local t-shirt/uniform shop.

Two, including the "old-timer", worked at the high school, one as the counselor and the other, a teacher and coach. And the sixth, and youngest, worked at the shirt shop, while finishing up his college degree.

Some of us played softball together in the summer. We played golf together. We went to Vegas together. We stayed out late together. (And we got in trouble with my wife one night together!)

But whatever we did, eventually the subject would usually come around to officiating. And not just "are you still officiating?" But talk about mechanics, or game situations, or odd plays, or the latest in equipment and uniforms. We would practice our signals on street corners. Or rehearse the next thing we are going to say to that smart-assed coach next year.

We were always double-checking our schedules to make sure who was going with whom and confirming dates for rules meetings. Or letting everyone know when there was an open date on our calendars.

Through a span of four or five years you rarely saw one of us at a game without another one with us. To be honest with you, it was great. We all pretty much had the same aspirations, the same abilities, the same philosophy as it related to game management, mechanics, and personality. And we were all pretty much available to work. Any trip under an hour to a game was a short night. It was not uncommon to put on 200-250 miles during a round trip somewhere.

We fed off of each other and knew enough to take care of each other when necessary. Very rarely did a coach, player, or fan say or do something some night that the both of us didn't know. We also got on each other when we knew someone screwed up, either on a mechanic or call or something that was said.

The other one generally heard about it on the way home and everyone else knew about it the next time that he worked with one of the other guys. But that closeness only made us all better. We all had different qualities that some others didn't have. Some of us were taller, some quicker, some louder, some got madder quicker, some could smile at the right time, some wittier, some more theatrical, but we could all work the games.

By the early 90's, post-season games for us were a regularity. Between the six of us it was not unusual for two or three of us to be going to the same regional or sub-state. The benefit of this was we were obviously familiar with each other and any game together would be easier to work mentally, if not physically.

Then it happened. Six letters from the activities association were delivered to Lyons' addresses that contained state tournament assignments. In 1991, the six of us were assigned to a state tournament in everything from Class 1A to 5A. Two of us, the pup and the old-timer, went to 1A and one each to 2A, 3A, 4A, and 5A.

The pup worked the front half of the 1A tournament in Hays. In fact, I and one of the other officials went to Hays to watch him work. The only problem was my car had a small brake malfunction on the way there and we didn't arrive until just after halftime. And his partner for that first state tournament game? None other than "Sonny" himself. The same "Sonny" that I had been paired with just three years earlier. Oh, I couldn't wait to hear the stories.

The rest of us worked the "back half" of our respective tournaments. For me, I made the three-hour trip to Topeka for the 5A tournament. As it turned out, I had a boy's semi-final game on Friday night and the girl's third place game on Saturday. My boy's semi-final featured Liberal, and sophomore phenom Martin Lewis, verses Ft Scott. Lewis was a 6'5" man-child who could knock down three-pointers or hammer tomahawk dunks. Lewis led Liberal into the final against McPherson as they played in front of nearly 7,000 fans in Topeka's Expocentre.

It was the practice of the activities association to print the names, and hometowns, of the officials working all state tournaments during this time. They produced one program that lists all the teams and games for each class at each tournament site. Looking at the list of officials in 1991, one would find that six officials came from the town of Lyons, more than any other city in the state. More than Topeka, more than Wichita, more than Kansas City. I was just as proud of seeing the other five names in that program as I was in seeing my own.

They have since dropped the practice of listing hometowns of the officials in the programs now, for obvious reasons. Nowadays, I doubt that Lyons even has six registered basketball officials. Of the six of us back then, none of us are still registered, for a variety of reasons. One is coaching in college, one is now a school administrator, some of us just got old and the pup is a successful professor in Missouri.

But during that year, the Lyons connection could hold its own with any city in the state and in any class.

IW'S
(INADVERTENT
WHISTLES)

Up to now, you have heard mostly about my basketball officiating from the beginning, as well as my formative years on the softball diamond. I guess now is as good a time as any to bring up my early exploits on the gridiron.

I can tell you that my first time refereeing a football game was the first time I ever stepped onto a football field for an actual game. No, I never played a down of football in my life. No youth league, no junior high, no high school, no college. Though there was a time when I seriously considered going out for football during my senior year of college to join my brother who was joining the team as a freshman. But that is another story for another time.

I did register with the activities association for a couple of years in the early 1980's, but that was mainly for show, thinking I might be interested, I really wasn't. But by 1988 I not only became more interested, I actually found some opportunities to work.

Now, I can't tell you if I had the chance to work any sub-varsity games or any scrimmages in order to find my comfort zone. I can tell you that my first varsity football game came that year in Wilson, Kansas. I was the line judge on the crew of four officials for this night. That in itself, considering my "experience" as a football official ,would qualify this night as an adventure.

My crew mates included a former football coach at Sterling College, and his son. This is the same football coach who I worked with early in my basketball career. Early on, things didn't go too badly, but then, at a point in the second quarter, on a sweep around the left end to my side of the field, came my defining moment. Someone on offense held a defensive player and the basketball official in me came out as soon as I saw it. Oh, I remembered to throw my flag alright – right after I blew my whistle.

Of course everyone stopped and wondered what was going on, me included. By rule, (which I admit, I didn't know then) we gave the offensive team the option of taking the ball where it was when I blew my inadvertent whistle or replaying the down. They took the play, and I took the whistle out of my mouth for a while.

Knowing now what I should have known then, I should never have stepped onto that field that night without some pre-season work. Normally these days that includes some scrimmage work, attending some kind of camp or clinic, and spending time with more seasoned officials learning and understanding the game. Oh, I guess I did all of that. It is just that it all happened during the 45-minute ride to the game. Hardly the kind of training work you would expect to see from less experienced officials today.

That all being said, I survived the night and went on to finish the season without any further incident. I hooked up with another crew the next year, although the word crew might be an exaggeration. It actually wound up being a group of six officials, with a vast difference in experience, ability, age, and outlook, with four different guys working each Friday night.

On this subsequent crew, I changed positions and moved to the umpire spot, just behind the defensive line. Again, back then all high school games in Kansas were officiated with just four officials. It would be some years before high school contests in Kansas would be officiated with a back judge on the crew.

I actually felt a lot more comfortable moving to the umpire spot. There was something to do on every play and getting to handle and spot the ball and interact with the players allowed me to stay involved and made me feel like I was doing something with every down. Games came and went and I began to feel comfortable with my new crew mates and my new position.

As the season went along, we were all looking forward to a game we had in Hays with Thomas More Prep and Larned. Not only was it going to be a game that matched a couple of pretty good teams at the time, but TMP played their home games at

Fort Hays State University, an experience we were all looking forward to.

Being able to work in what is normally a college atmosphere was an experience we were all excited about. Looking back today there was not any one thing that stood out about that game compared to any other game we had that season . . . except one thing. Well, two things actually.

In the second quarter, Larned was on a drive to score an apparent touchdown. After moving the ball inside the 10 yard line, Larned ran a play just off of the left tackle. As the running back turned up field, just inside the left tackle, he broke through to cross the goal line. At least I thought it was the goal line. As he crossed the line and I blew my whistle, it was then I realized that he had crossed the five-yard line.

So we give Larned their options for my inadvertent whistle and they choose to run the play over.

Which they proceed to do only this time instead of giving the ball to the running back just inside the left tackle, they take the ball outside the tackle around the left end. Somewhere between my efforts to make sure that the running back inside the tackle 1) didn't have the ball and 2) if he did I didn't blow it dead before he got to the goal line, the running back outside the end, did have the ball, turned up field and . . . well, you guessed it.

At that point I left my whistle out of my mouth for the remainder of the half. This could not end soon enough, for me or my crew.

You know those Southwest Airline commercials where the person has screwed up and is looking for a place to run and hide? That was me. But out there in the middle of the football field there is no place to run and no place to hide. At least not until we can get to the locker room at halftime. And then, you can only stay there for 15 minutes before having to go out and face the music again. And I couldn't go out there for the second half without my whistle, no matter how much I tried or how many times my crew mates made the suggestion.

Who knows, maybe that is why mechanics change; why now we put so much emphasis on umpires in football not blowing their whistles. At least I am sure that I sped up the movement in that direction. Needless to say, my football exploits have improved since then. At least I hope they have.

Of course, how could they not?

THE METRO, NBC, AND BASEBALL

The final piece of my officiating puzzle was baseball. I did not get into baseball umpiring until right after I graduated from college. Mainly because I was still working some softball and, at least around Sterling, there was not much baseball to be call. Only a few of the larger high schools in that part of the state played baseball. That left college baseball in the spring.

While in college at Sterling, I kept stats for the college baseball team for a couple of years and ran across a couple of umpires during the spring who I was working softball with. They were the ones who got me interested in the idea of working baseball. Most of those guys were out of the Wichita area. They not only worked games at Sterling, but at several other colleges in that same conference, as well as some junior colleges in the area. Their organization was called the Metro Umpires Association (MUA).

So after college I called one of the umpires in the organization to find out what I needed to do to get involved with baseball. It wasn't anything too hard. Pay a $15 fee and purchase the necessary shirts and pants required by the organization. I also needed to go to Wichita and attended a pre-season clinic at which time a lot of the games in the spring would be assigned.

Now this is the early 1980's. One reason the Metro even existed was because they represented a group of umpires that pulled out of what was then the Wichita Umpires Association. In doing that, they felt they needed to identify themselves so schools and teams would not think this was the old WUA.

Back then, and to some extent even today, the National Baseball Congress World Series is the biggest baseball event in the Midwest. Held each August and bringing semi-pro teams from all over the country to Wichita for a national championship. NBC umpires at the time wore red shirts with the navy blue pants. So to distinguish themselves from the NBC and the WUA, the Metro went with . . . are you ready? Orange shirts and royal blue pants. (Go ahead; take your time while that picture sinks in.)

By that time, the Metro also was able to make inroads and take on the umpiring duties of the NBC World Series. Other umpires were used, but the Metro umpires got the majority of the games. I umpired six games my first year working the NBC tournament. Even though we were still dressing out of our cars at most venues, I was beginning to feel like I was finding a home on the baseball diamond.

Umpiring in the NBC tournament was not exactly like getting the assignment for the Major League World Series. It was more like who was available. Using umpires primarily from the Wichita area, any umpire who contacted the NBC about the tournament could qualify. Over the years, umpires came from Alaska, California, Texas, New York, Oklahoma and Michigan. It wasn't so much that umpires from outside the area were not welcome, umpires just were not paid well enough for most to want to come to Wichita for several days at their own expense, for $40 per game in the mid 80's.

Eventually the pay got somewhat better. By the time I finished working the tournament around 2002, umpires were getting $75 per game. I put in 20 years working the NBC tournament each August. For me, it got to a point where I just wasn't enjoying myself as much as I used to and felt it was time for me to step aside and let some of the younger guys carry on.

When I started with the tournament, Carl Lewton of Carthage, Missouri, was the Supervisor of Umpires. He was working with the NBC on mechanics, rules and assignment of umpires. By this time Carl was up there in age, but he still managed to work a game or two in the tournament when necessary. He served as supervisor for 24 years, before being inducted into the NBC Hall of Fame in 1996.

Carl, a high school coach and teacher in Carthage, not only worked with the NBC, but he also conducted umpire clinics around Missouri as well as Mexico and Venezuela. In fact, the baseball diamond in Carthage, a former minor league park back in the KOM (Kansas, Oklahoma, and Missouri) League days of Mickey Mantle, is named after Carl.

Carl always treated me fairly. I believe he appreciated the fact that I was always on time, ready to work when called upon, and didn't embarrass myself, the NBC, or him when it was all said and done. Not everyone felt the same way about Carl. Sure he was a little quirky. But who isn't when they reach their 70's? Carl passed away in October of 2009, but I am forever grateful for the opportunities he gave me during those summers in Wichita.

Eventually, my baseball began to consist of mostly NCAA Division II and NAIA college baseball in Kansas during the spring. I also eventually worked high school baseball as well and have been lucky enough to work a couple of state high school baseball tournaments in Kansas and in Colorado.

My summers these days generally consist of some club baseball. Not a lot, but just enough games during June and July to work a couple of games each week. (And help pay for an ever-increasing golf habit.) I always enjoy the single-game nights that the summer offers, but do not regret my decision to step away from the mid-August NBC tournament. I'll leave those 105 degree days on the turf for the young guys.

And it was baseball that attracted my wife to me. At least that is what she says. I was heavily involved with the NBC tournament when we started going together and she loved going to baseball games – still does. I think she misses the tournament more than I do. I know she enjoyed visiting with Carl's wife, Lois, as well.

Maybe it has something to do with age. Maybe we can blame it on climate change. Maybe the baseball just isn't as good as it once was. Whatever it is, I still love going to the diamond, I love working games, but some days I love seeing the diamond in my rear view mirror on my way home more.

IT'S TIME TO MOVE

Working as the Superintendent of Recreation in Lyons, Kansas provided me with the opportunities I needed at the time; a steady job in a field I enjoyed, enough flexibility to continue officiating, and a community and part of the state I was comfortable in.

I remember thinking when I was growing up in Sterling that I would never leave Sterling. It provided everything for me I needed. But then I moved to Lyons. Then I remember thinking that I would never leave Lyons. But, in 1992, my wife and I left Lyons and moved to Topeka.

I felt I had taken the job with the recreation commission as far as I could, or as far as it was going to carry me. My thoughts were that I was going to need something new or I was going to be in Lyons for a long, long time. That being said, an opportunity to go to work for the American Heart Association in the area of fundraising as an Area Director became a reality. After originally applying for a position to be located in Dodge City, the organization offered me a similar position out of the main office in Topeka.

Moving to Topeka not only meant finding a new home, new friends, and new surroundings, but also a new officiating schedule. In actuality, the officiating schedule was probably the easiest of all. Between my previous experience in state basketball tournaments, ASA softball, and some experience at the college level, I had several contacts in Topeka that could help me along.

Of course, it wasn't easy. By not making the move until after July 4th, that really made it difficult jumping into the football and basketball seasons, since most, if not all of the games would already assigned. But I was able to use some of my contacts to help me get my foot in the door that first year.

As for football, I was able to work eight out of nine Friday nights of the high school varsity season for someone somewhere, filling in at one of the four positions. Coming from Lyons, I had spent most of my limited football career working as an umpire, with just some spot duty later on as the referee, though it began that fateful night in Wilson on the wing.

As luck would have it, I finished the season working as an umpire for a crew I had filled in for before. On that final week of the regular season, the normal umpire was in the process of moving to southwest Kansas for a new job. Being as there were a couple of officials on this crew who I had some basketball experience with, they asked me to join them full time for the next football season.

That continued to be the same crew, more or less, for 20 years in Topeka. Crews in Kansas have since gone to five officials for high school football, adding a back judge in the late 1990's, with all leagues in northeast Kansas adopting five-man crews by 2000. Going into the 2010 season, three of us had formed the nucleus of this crew. Others would come and go in later years, but we made the effort to keep the crew together through guys coming and going, kids playing high school football, retirements, etc. Sometime during the move from four officials to five, I moved from umpire to referee, where I remained.

As for basketball, I used a lot of the same contacts to help me develop a schedule. I was able to help fill some holes and, as is the life of an official, someone is always getting hurt. The uncertainty of it all causes as much apprehension as anything. If a guy can get over that, then the rest is gravy.

Of course, after six straight state basketball tournaments, that string came to an end. I did make it to sub-state and was satisfied with that considering I spent the year working with new partners, new coaches, and new schools and commissioners.

Through the moving process, you find that different areas do things differently. Even though I stayed within the state of Kansas, it was different moving from Lyons (or as some in the eastern part of the state would consider, "Western Kansas") to Topeka, the state capital. My expectations were fairly high considering what I thought I knew.

As it turned out, even though there were more officials, more schools, and more games, there were still just as many, in percentage, of officials who were adequate at best, schools and coaches who were difficult to work for, and games and teams you dreaded working. What I expected in an overall improved quality in the game in general did not meet my expectations.

What was different was a philosophy about the game. Oh, it was still the same game with the same desired outcome, but how we got there was not. And as I would later find out, Kansas is not alone.

I GOT A 6A (AGAIN)

The whole process for an official, any official, is to be able to work the big games, to be called upon to be there on "that" night, to know that others have confidence in you to get the job done.

The process of assigning officials to "big" games during the regular season typically falls upon the shoulders of assignors of some sort, regardless of the sport. They may be league assignors, association assignors, individual officials contracted by the teams or schools, or athletic directors themselves. In just about every case, it is a thankless job.

Each assignor has his or her own math or science to make the process manageable. But regardless of whether there are 10 games or 1,000, it is not a perfect process. It involves the ability to manage some logistics, attitudes, personal schedules and preferences, and a lot of just plain old blind faith. And some phone calls. Usually a lot of phone calls. Even in today's age of assigning systems such as Arbiter.

But as I described before, the process of post-season assignments for high school contests in Kansas in the mid 90's generally involved the US Postal Service. And sometimes a fax machine and sometimes a phone call.

As I also mentioned some chapters ago, the anticipation of post-season games became a highlight for me during the years. That was especially true as far as basketball was concerned, but was also the case for me involving any sport. This time though, having been in Topeka and just finishing my sixth year of working games in that part of the state, the entire process had the same feel that it had when I was just starting out back in Lyons.

So as the timing came for those letters to arrive for the various levels of post-season play, the mailbox again got a lot of my attention. Everyone knew when the letters and assignments for sub-state came out. So having that in my mailbox not only provided a sense that I had been rewarded for a good season, but also a sense of accomplishment knowing that not everyone who wanted an assignment got one, or at the very least, one that they felt they deserved. My sub-state assignment for this particular year was a 5A tournament held at a school in Topeka.

Though the assignment of teams and officials had been tweaked over the years just prior to this, the basic format remained the same. But because I was still working tournaments in the western part of the state, in Hays and Dodge City during the year, when the chance came to have either boys or girls teams from there it felt like the powers that be from the KSHSAA office made that happen, whether they came east or I went west. This particular year Hays came east, 200 miles east to Topeka, for sub-state.

So, as the sub-state week came around, again officials were hopeful for what may come to their mailboxes. This time though, only a total of 144 basketball officials would get that all-anticipated mailing from the KSHSAA office.

And I'll be damned! On Friday I received just such a mailing. Could this possibly be something else that the office was sending out? Baseball rule books? Official's handbook? Anything else? Only one way to find out. Open it up and let's see.

And there was that same familiar heading:

TO: Class 6A State Basketball Officials

SITE: White Auditorium, Emporia

HOST: Emporia Sports Commission

"You have been selected to officiate in the Class 6A State Basketball Tournament listed above. To accept this assignment, please complete the form enclosed and return it to the KSHSAA office immediately. If you cannot accept this assignment, please contact our office immediately at . . . "

It had taken me six years, basically the same amount of time it had when I first started out, to get back to the state tournament. Now understand, post-season assignments in Kansas were dictated based on the number of recommendations you received from coaches at the end of the season. This particular year, I received 18 recommendations from basketball coaches. Enough to get me back to the first two days (Wednesday & Thursday) of the tournament. I was going to the 6A state basketball tournament.

Like sub-state tournaments, assignments from the KSHSAA office for state tournaments try to follow the same criteria and reasoning as to when and where officials are assigned. (i.e. recommendations) As it turned out, I did have teams and coaches whom I was familiar and very comfortable with. My Wednesday girl's game was Blue Valley North vs. Hutchinson. The Hutchinson coach was a guy I went to college with and had stayed in touch with all those years. He had been the girls coach at Hutchinson for some time and really turned that team around. My Thursday boy's game was Dodge City vs. Kansas City Schlagel. Both of these coaches I was very familiar with, having officiated the TOC in Dodge City going on 20 years with Schlagel a regular every other year participant. Both games went by without incident and it was a great feeling to be back in familiar territory.

For me, even though I was still working a few college games during this time, I was rewarded with a post-season assignment that I knew I was worthy of. As an official, that is all we can ask for and all we can hope for.

Life is good again.

FIVE

Regardless of the circumstances, or the situation, everyone wishes to be liked, admired and wanted. We also believe that we are capable of doing the job that is required of us. This is especially true of sports officials.

Officials have to have some ego. And those who climb to the top of any level need to have a little more. That, along with a thick skin. And a short memory. And confidence in themselves that what they are doing is the right thing.

That being said, officials must also adapt to certain situations and be willing to look at themselves in the mirror with the understanding that influences and influencers come from a variety of sources.

Inside the core of any official is an understanding of how the game is to be played and how it is to be officiated. Beyond that, an official learns what works and what doesn't and tries to put it all together in a package that is reflective of who they are. That, in the end, is what helps identify officials; good ones, bad ones, those who are out for the money, and those who are out for themselves.

And with that, comes feedback. Feedback from coaches, players, administrators. Feedback from assigners, organizations, and leagues. Feedback from partners, fellow officials, and those who watch the games.

This feedback comes in a variety of ways. The most obvious to an official is in his or her schedule, through the total number, quality, and the level of games. It also comes in the quality of the officials with whom one gets to work.

Feedback can also come through in something a little more concrete. In some cases, this feedback could include written evaluations and reports. In some higher levels this can also include a video review of recent contests. And in some instances, such as camps and clinics, it would include a one-on-one sit down to thoroughly review the good, the bad, and the ugly.

Regardless of how the feedback is presented, it is how it is received that will ultimately be the determining factor in how much, how soon, and how well an official improves. In the end, that is ultimately what the goal is; to improve officials and improve officiating.

I am not, nor have I ever been, immune from any of the above feedback; Everything from anger and disgust from coaches, players, and administrators; After games from partners and observers; And one-on-one from clinicians, assigners, and those at the higher levels.

And in each instance, I, as should any official, must take that feedback, digest it, and determine just how it would, or could, make me a better official. In a best case scenario, no official could be expected to take an entire review and turn it around to fit his or her game. Instead, an official would be best to take bits and pieces, the lower fruit if you will, and fit it into what is already working; but hanging on to all of it, especially if the feedback continues to repeat itself time and time again.

Though how much we try, the feedback may not always be in a form that can provide much direction. In these cases, it is up to the individual official to look within and to make sense of it all, deciding ultimately just how to make it work.

As I have mentioned before, the biggest area of feedback used by KSHSAA is recommendations from coaches. This is true for all sports, from football and volleyball in the fall, to basketball and wrestling in the winter, to baseball and softball in the spring.

This format of recommendations from coaches evolved during my years as an official in Kansas. My first year, 1980, the state association would provide cards for officials to give coaches for their use after the completion of each varsity game. These cards listed criteria like knowledge of rules, dress, professionalism, and use of signals. Each official was to be evaluated on each criterion on a scale of one through five. The varsity coach, upon completing the card, would then send it to the state office as required. From here, the state office would compile the cards received and make assignments for post-season contests as they saw fit. Then things changed.

From 1981 until the present, head coaches at each school provide a list of officials who they feel are capable of working post-season contests. No explanation, no ranking by numbers, just a list of names. With a minimum of 10 names required, up to a total of 15.

And it is by those numbers, the total recommendations received from coaches each season, that the association would decide which officials, where, and how many will work each post-season for each sport. The more recommendations, the more games you worked. The more recommendations, the further through the post-season you advanced. The concept being, the most recommended officials would work the most games and, ultimately, the most important games, i.e. the state finals.

Again, as the regular season would draw to a close, officials would always try to estimate where they were regarding the number of recommendations they expected to receive. And when the regular season was completed and early round post-season games were assigned, it would be a regular occurrence for individual officials to contact the association office and inquire as the total number of recommendations received.

Before computers, and long before officiating software like Arbiter, I can only guess the piles of paperwork, coaches cards, and lists of officials with their total recommendations listed that were kept in the state office. The only thing that I could relate it to would be like my early years as a commissioner for our fantasy football league, long before websites like Yahoo or CBS Sports, in which everything had to be kept by paper and pencil and you had to get the stats out of the Monday paper to see who won or lost the slate of fantasy games for the weekend.

And I, like every other official in the state, would make that call to the state office, get transferred to the appropriate person based on the sport and check on our recommendations.

It did not matter which sport, football, basketball, baseball, or any other, the state office knew to expect those calls.

As officials, we always would try and estimate what that number would be before we called. You could go through your schedule and look back at the teams and coaches you had, the type of games you had, and decide who you thought would, or would not put your name on their recommendation list. The truth being, you might get close on the number, but the reality of it was you could never really be sure who did or did not put your name on that list. Despite whatever chit-chat you had with a coach before, during, or after games, it would still be just a guess.

So after finally getting back to a state tournament six years after moving to Topeka, I was again anticipating this time of year. Post-season assignments for basketball were on the way and the guessing game had begun. Where was I going, who was I going to work, and who was I going to be working with?

This time my letter indicated that I was going to Junction City to work a Class 6A Sub-State and I was going to work the boy's final on Saturday. As it turned out, that game would be between Wichita Heights and Wichita East. Those same powerful city-league teams that continue to meet so often during the Tournament of Champions. So I fill out my paperwork to accept this upcoming assignment and prepare to take it by the state office later the next day and pose the inevitable question.

I stop by the office with my paperwork, and ask to see Paul (Paul Palmer, the assistant responsible for basketball). I hand him my papers, engage in some idle chit-chat and finally ask him the question. How many recommendations did I get?

His response, "Do you really want to know?"

"Sure," I reply.

"Five," he says.

At that point, I don't honestly remember any more of the conversation. I do remember getting in my car. And being mad!

Not really sure at who. Myself? My partners? Coaches? The state association? My games? Five! I could get five recommendations sitting in the stands at a junior high tournament, I thought to myself.

I worked the set of sub-state games that next week, knowing I would be finishing my season there, feeling that I was a better official than my outcome; and deciding then how I would approach future assignments.

I knew then that my approach to officiating was for the wrong reasons. I was working to get post-season assignments. What I needed to be doing was working the games to the best of my ability and let the results fall where they may. I knew I could work. It was up to everyone else to figure that out. From that point on, I was working to satisfy myself and my conscience and know that my best was good enough for me.

Too bad it took me nearly 20 years to figure it out. Some never figure it out. But that season of five recommendations made me a better official.

IT IS BECOMING A FULL-TIME JOB (I HAVE BECOME AN OFFICIATING WHORE!)

Officials, by and large, want to work games. Trust me when I say that officials get a rush from calling games. The bigger the game, the bigger the rush. All officials look ahead on their schedule to see where, who, and with whom they will be working. For some, the essential motive could be money. For some it could be their interest and love of the sport. And then again, it could be the thrill of being in control.

For me, it was the idea of knowing that each team was going to get a fair chance to compete. Obviously, there have been many times when the outcome could be expected. But I cannot recall any time when I worked a game and my calls or personal preference made a difference in the outcome. Sure, did a call not go the way someone wanted it? It happens every game. But an official's call or no call does not determine the outcome of a game.

That is not to say that I never made a call that proved to be decisive in the outcome of the game. But it was a call that was required, based on what was happening in the game at the time. It may have been an out on base or a called strike. It may have been a foul or violation on one team or player. In any case, there are too many other decisions in the game, made by officials, players and coaches, that have an impact on the game long before any decision I, or any other official, have to make in the final moments.

But my point is that all officials are motivated in one way or another to work games. Sometimes it can be lots of games. That was true for me as well.

There were some basketball seasons where I worked in excess of 80 games. This included varsity games, high school, college, sub-varsity, junior high, even holiday alumni games. In fact, there was January 1992, where I worked 28 games over 21 days that month. When I was deep in my basketball career, it would begin the first week of November and end the second week of March.

When I was working three sports (football, basketball and baseball), basketball was my number one sport. My officiating schedule revolved around what I was doing during the basketball season. There was one occurrence in early March while living in Lyons, when I worked a college baseball doubleheader at Sterling College in the afternoon and a high school sub-state basketball boys final at the college that night. (Okay, maybe I did have one more double-dip in me.) But beyond that, if my basketball schedule interfered at any point, my baseball schedule would just have to wait. But when basketball was over, it was full-speed-ahead with baseball.

Baseball would remain in full swing from mid-March until early August. That meant high school and college games in the early spring from March through May. Then would come the nights of summer baseball, which for a long time ended with the NBC tournament in August.

There were the few times that baseball did run up against the football calendar. It happened a couple of times for me in Kansas and once or twice in Colorado as well. For the most part, it meant that final summer season baseball games (World Series caliber games, either NBC or Little League) won out over pre-season football conflicts. Those conflicts on the football side were generally pre-season rules meetings or the like. But that meant that in order to get those in I would have to plan on some extra travel to make those meetings. But there were also times during the season, especially in Kansas, that because of my job responsibilities, I needed to attend required officiating meetings outside of my regular area of northeast Kansas in general and Topeka specifically.

I attended an area supervisor meeting for football in Garden City once, nearly 300 miles from my home in Topeka. Also, while in Topeka, I attended basketball meetings in Colby, Wichita, Salina, Hays, Great Bend and Dodge City. I even attended a volleyball area supervisor's meeting in Colby one year, just to learn and advance as an official, even though I was only registered for volleyball for two years.

There was a fallback in Kansas that let an official take a separate test, referred to as Test 2, when meetings were missed.

I never did use that as an option. I made my scheduled travel work. I had always heard that Test 2 was hard.

Even in Colorado, after my officiating career began to wind down considerably, I needed to make arrangements to travel to Pueblo or Denver or Canon City, knowing I would miss the required meeting scheduled in Colorado Springs.

I completed and mailed my football test for Kansas one summer from my mother-in-law's house on the lake in Minnesota. I completed the same test on a computer while in Iowa for sprint car races. I drove nearly 500 miles round trip back to Topeka from a business retreat at Lake of the Ozarks in Missouri to work a high school all-star basketball game. For free! I missed the final day of a state park and recreation conference in Manhattan to drive back to Wichita for a college women's basketball game.

I found ways to make my travel schedule work for me while with the American Heart Association. Knowing that I would be going to Hays or Dodge City for basketball tournaments during the season, I would schedule necessary visits with contacts in the area for my down time during the day and referee the games at night.

At some point while in Topeka, one of my regular football and basketball partners referred to me as an "officiating whore". After thinking about it for a couple of seconds, I agreed with him. I am not sure how or when it started. Or why. But I would imagine it happens to a lot of officials at one time or another.

In other words, we want or crave officiating so much, that we essentially "sell" ourselves professionally. We (I) become addicted. It really does become a full-time job. Between the meetings and the tests and the rules review, it takes time and dedication. And that's before the games even start. The games just take it to a whole other level.

For some, the addiction may last for years. Mine did. For others, it may be the main reason for stopping. But if a person really likes officiating and really wants to continue to work at a high level, they have to become "an officiating whore". They sell themselves for the next game, for the next season, for the next opportunity.

Doing so though means you have a family that understands. And a job (and a boss) that is compatible. But sometimes we tend to forget.

I HAD NO IDEA

As I mentioned in the previous chapter, family is a large part of any official's success, regardless of whether you work youth league or sub-varsity games or find yourself at the major college level or the professional ranks.

Officials spend a considerable amount of time away from home and family activities. Not only do they spend time working games, but there is the time spent in meetings, at clinics, doing rules study or completing tests, traveling to and from game sites, and cleaning, repairing, and replacing equipment.

Regarding equipment, there always seems to be a juggling act when it comes to where I put my equipment. Working three sports for most of my officiating career, closet space always seems to be at a premium, though there is some overlap between sports. I use the same shoes for football as I do for baseball on the bases. Most of my undergarments can go from sport to sport. But beyond that, that is pretty much where the sharing ends.

So my closet is filled with striped shirts for football, striped shirts for basketball, and the obligatory color palette of shirts for baseball. (Let's see, there is navy blue with two state association logos and those without. Powder blue with and without logos for high school and college. Two styles of black shirts with three types of logos and some without. Then there is white with dark blue collar, cream, and then some with long sleeves. Oh yea, there are two black jackets and one navy blue. And one still very useful, in Colorado at least, navy blue plate coat.) At least the charcoal gray pants can transfer across state lines and associations.

Then there is the equipment and the necessary bags to carry it all. Some suitcases pull double duty between certain seasons and vacation travel, however, my baseball bag really only serves a single function. And when it is not in use, it takes up the entire bottom of the closet.

Shoes have always been a priority of mine since I began working games in my teens. My biggest issue with shoes has been the fact that I wear a size 15. Early on, in my initial softball days, I actually went without plate shoes for the first few years due to the fact that I could never find a pair big enough. That was before the internet, before national chain sporting goods stores, and before officiating supply warehouses.

Not only are my feet big, but they are flat as well. So shoes and insoles remain important since the sports I work require being constantly on your feet and running more often than not. Plus, when you stick a pair of size 15's in your bag (or two for baseball) it doesn't take long to fill it up.

In the early days, I spent a lot of time keeping my shoes cleaned and polished. Thankfully, along came patent leather. Then the quality of the leather also got better and so did the options for keeping shoes cleaned and looking like new. (Thank you Armor All, Scrubbing Bubbles, Aqua Net Hair Spray, and artificial turf.)

Of course, the packing and repacking before and after games takes time. Then there is loading it up in the car and dragging it to the dressing room, though most local baseball fields mean dressing out of your car trunk or the back of your SUV. Then that also means taking along a folding chair of some kind. And something to stand on besides the dirt and rocks of the parking lot. And a small ice chest with something to drink.

You can try and leave everything in the back of the car or SUV for a few days when you can, but then it seems like the grand kids have to go somewhere or we need to go to the grocery store or my golf clubs have to stand in the corner of the garage.

So an official's life always seems to cross paths with everyday life; with mom or the wife, with the job, with the home, with vacations, with special dates, with other events. With everyone's emotions.

When my wife and I were married in 1988, I had already been officiating for more than half of my life. As I mentioned before, that is how we met. I worked recreation league softball and basketball games for her and her boss, who was an official some 10-12 years earlier. I had also become very routine in my preparation, not only before games, but after as well and the day or days leading up to the next assignment.

My wife not only knew that I officiated, as I said, she liked going to most of my games as well. (Except for football. She hates football.) So it was not uncommon for her to tag along to basketball games and weekend baseball. We made a lot of friends at a variety of locations that we saw, and still see, years later through my game assignments.

Of course, games do not always go as we hope. And on the court or the field there is a different perspective. Despite what fans say, there is a reason why officials are on the playing surface with the competitors and not sitting in the stands. On the field/court, you interact with the players and coaches. You hear what is said to you and around you. Some if it is harmless. Some of it is sarcastic. And some of it is just plain stupid. But after years of working games and knowing what happens in certain situations, you hear it all. Thus the necessity for the thick skin.

Baseball, due to the fact that the fans are so far away from the direct action on the field, lends itself to those interactions that most people watching do not recognize or pay attention to. Conversations happen all the time that even to the trained eye, appear harmless. Good umpires turn their back to the stands so that the conversation carries out to the outfield. And with enclosed dugouts, especially those built in the ground, verbal jousting from players and coaches have no chance to be heard in the stands. Thus, a perfect storm struck one day during one of my last NBC tournaments.

One Saturday, I was scheduled to work at 1 pm and 4:30 pm. It so happened that my oldest stepson was with us that day. Actually, he had come to Topeka from South Carolina where he and I went to Iowa for a couple of days for some sprint car races. As a result, we had gotten home really late

Friday night/Saturday morning. After about four hours of sleep, he, his mother and I made the two-hour trip to Wichita from Topeka for my two games.

My first game was on the plate and turned out to be a no-hitter by the winning pitcher. My stepson, a photographer and graphic artist, took several pictures that day. One is of me working the plate. We have that photo hanging in our house still today. My wife (his mom) loves the picture so we had it enlarged and framed.

My second game was on the bases. Neither game seemed to be too terribly tough to work. But, it was August in Kansas, on a turf field, working two games, and the before mentioned constant chatter from the dugouts. As you might imagine, everyone was glad to walk off the diamond when it was all said and done.

So when I got to our car, a Dodge Durango at the time, my wife and stepson were there ready to go. After loading my equipment and clothes, I crawled into the driver's seat. That is one thing that never changed over all my years of officiating and marriage. I always drive. (Except for that one time coming home from Concordia when she did drive and I made her stop the car so I could get out and throw up. But that is another story.)

From the diamond in Wichita to the highway home was typically thirty minutes before finally getting to highway speed for the next 120 miles. During that time the conversation usually centered on the game, any special events that occurred or did not occur, anything my wife heard or saw in the stands, and are we going to stop and get something to eat and/or drink, and if so where.

It was during these 30 minutes through Wichita to the highway, in August, in 100 plus degree heat, after two games on an artificial turf field that my nerves remained on edge. By the time we get to the highway, my stepson, sitting in the passenger seat in front, still had his window down. By the time we get up to 70 plus on the highway and the window still isn't up, I snapped.

"Roll that damn window up!!!!"

I caught him glance back at his mom. Then he rolled the window up. The next several miles were pretty quiet. We stopped soon after for a bite to eat. When we get back in the car, he goes to the back seat and she moved to the front.

We get home and we all go about our business. I have clothes to wash, my stepson is working on his plans for his return trip home back in South Carolina, and my wife cornered me. I basically heard all about my attitude and how I handled the situation.

Without going into the gory details, she was right and I had no idea. I had actually forgotten about my comments by the time we were home. My stepson and my wife had not. They had talked about it when we stopped to eat. I was, as was customary, in my own little world after the game. But in no uncertain terms, she quickly reminded me that when I was in the car, I was not dealing with players or coaches any more.

Truth be known, it was probably not the first time that the game carried over into the ride home. But it was the first time that it carried over into someone other than my wife. It just happened this time to be her son.

But that is the slippery slope we officials must constantly navigate. We still talk about it in meetings today. We do not take what happens at home or work onto the court/field with us. Conversely we should not take what happens on the court/field back home.

My wife is different than most officials' wives in that she was an official herself when we were married and knew of my love of officiating long before. Plus she does love most sports as much and sometimes more than I do. So she understands the officials' life and his or her thoughts and dilemmas. But she also knew, this time, it crossed the line.

To my knowledge, it has not happened since. Or at least not to the extent that she has needed to intervene again. Oh sure, officiating has conflicted with the family personal schedule, but those are the things that you just have to work through. But that day is a reminder to just how fine the line is between being an official and being a husband, or father, or co-worker. I know some who do struggle with the distinction. Some bounce from job to job to make officiating work. Not all marriages last.

Thankfully, ours has.

BECOMING AN AREA SUPERVISOR FOR UNCLE PAUL

Throughout the state of Kansas, the activities association uses a format of area supervisors to conduct meetings and relay information across the state to officials in a variety of sports. Some sports have more area supervisors than others. Some only cover a small metropolitan area, while some cover the greater part of western Kansas.

The idea being that officials can go to area supervisor meetings in their part of the state to get the latest updates and rulings from the state office, discuss situations that have risen, and better themselves as they progress through the season, leading up to post-season games. Area supervisor meetings in Kansas were, and still are, a requirement for officials wishing to work post-season games.

Typically, meetings are designated as Area I, Area II, and Area III (if necessary). An Area I meeting would generally take place on Monday at one location and on Wednesday at a different location or city. The Area I meetings would also take place right before the start of the season. So an official would actually have two opportunities to attend this Area I meeting. The same information, received by the area supervisor from the activities association, would be discussed at each of the meetings.

The general requirement is that officials interested in working post-season games would need to make one meeting from each round. Area II meetings would also be conducted on two days during a week at a point after the first third of the season. Area III meetings would then be closer to the end of the regular season, again, as officials look forward to the post-season.

Attendance is taken by the area supervisor at the meeting, which more often than not would be conducted in a school classroom somewhere in the designated city. Part of the area supervisor's responsibility is to confirm those meeting locations, generally, over the summer, so that the appropriate information can be sent to officials prior to the start of the season. Meetings would typically last around 90 minutes, covering questions on rules and providing mechanics information the state sees necessary.

Now, since these meetings are only required for post-season eligibility, not all officials feel compelled to attend. And it is not because the information presented is for the upper level or more seasoned officials. It is due to the fact that some officials are not interested in post-season games. Or, I am afraid, some officials are not interested in learning and getting better. It has always been my contention that these area meetings should be required for any official who desires working regular season varsity games. I started going as soon as I become registered to do so for each sport, necessary or not.

That being said, attendance at these meetings was always pretty good. Generally, you could always count on 20-30 for sure. Some meetings in Topeka would reach the 50-60 range during basketball season.

If you remember me mentioning earlier that I attended meetings in a variety of locations around the state of Kansas, it was for these types of meetings. Besides the fact that officials could attend a meeting outside of his or her designated area, it also gave them the opportunity to learn from a different presenter.

And these area supervisors were selected by the person at the activities association responsible for that particular sport. In many cases, it was not unusual to have the same area supervisor for football and basketball. Also, more often than not, these area supervisors were working officials. Often, you would see these officials work deep into the post-season as well. So they were not only respected by the activities association, but by the coaches as well.

When I first registered with the activities association for basketball for the 1979-80 season that was my first introduction to these meetings. My schedule that first year was filled with only junior high and sub-varsity games. However, I was interested enough in getting better that I took the time to attend these meetings right from the start. So I made that trip, while still in college, from Sterling to Hutchinson to attend basketball area meetings conducted by John Summerville.

Maybe because he was my first; maybe because I wound up going to more of John's meetings that any other area supervisor; or maybe because John was an educator in real life, for whatever the reason, I believe John was the best at what he did for those that I attended on a regular basis. He encouraged discussion. He answered all questions. And if he didn't know the answer, which was rare, he would say so, but he would find out.

As it turned out, John also was the area supervisor for football in this area. As it also turned out, which I did not know at the time, John was a Division I football official and still working high school basketball. In fact I worked with John in one of the last high school basketball games he officiated. But like any good mentor, John did not carry himself above any other official. I believe his first interest was in trying to make everyone else better.

Good officials will tell you that you never stop learning. Even today, I make the effort to attend meetings, required or not, to pick something up. Rules, even back in 1980, were complicated and required some digging into the rule book to find the right answer. Mechanics change as well. And getting together and hearing the same information helps put everyone on the same page.

So when I left Lyons and moved to Topeka, I left the comfort of the Summerville meetings. In Topeka, Jeff Stromgren gave the meetings for both football and basketball. As it turned out, I soon joined Jeff on his high school football crew. Jeff, in turn, was also a very accomplished basketball official. Shortly after I moved to Topeka, Jeff began moving up the ladder in basketball and moved onto Division 1 women's games. He would sneak in the occasional high school game, but with D-1 coaches in the stands from time to time, Jeff needed to step down from his supervisor responsibilities for basketball.

When Jeff stepped down, the association went outside Topeka for its basketball area supervisor. Chosen was a very accomplished official, who had worked many state tournaments. In fact, I worked with this official in a couple of state tournaments myself. But after a few years, the meetings began to take on a very apathetic and negative attitude. After one meeting in Lawrence, in which there were only about 12 in attendance, I decided I was going into the association office to discuss my feelings with the current director of basketball, Paul Palmer.

Paul had seen me work. He had taken over the position with the association from longtime assistant director Kaye Pearce, who had moved on to the executive director position, before soon retiring. Honestly, I would not have gone in to see Paul, if I did not feel he would listen to what I had to say.

When I sat down in his office, I right away said I was not coming in wanting to take on the job of area supervisor. But I thought he needed to know that the meetings had turned into nothing more than criticism of the association and the personal feelings of the area supervisor. I told him, if I had been sitting close enough to the door of that classroom in Lawrence, I would have walked out of the meeting. I felt that we were there to learn, but no one was learning anything that would help us become better officials. Paul listened, asked questions, and took notes. I thanked him for his time and for the opportunity to get some things off of my chest. I finished the season, saw Paul a few other times before the year was over, and moved on to baseball thereafter.

Sometime during that spring Paul called. He wanted to know if I would be interested in being the next area supervisor for basketball. After some discussion about what actually needed to be done and what the real responsibilities and duties were, I accepted. Other than my discussions with Paul, few others knew of the decision. However, when the packets went out for basketball sometime in October, everyone knew.

Actually, Stromgren knew and at some time during the summer, he wanted to know if I would be interested in taking on the football responsibilities as well. Though interested, I told him to let me get through this first year with basketball and I would let him know. I felt comfortable enough that first year with the responsibilities of being an area supervisor for basketball. I didn't feel comfortable enough to tackle football as well.

And, boy, did I hear it from some of the local guys then. Especially from some of my regular partners, who were also on the same football crew with Jeff and me. Pretty soon, every time we saw each other, they would inquire, "How is Uncle Paul?", referencing that I was now part of the association family and that Uncle Paul would take care of me now during basketball season. Despite what most think, that was not the case. At least it wasn't for me and I do not believe it was for anyone else either.

I had learned a few things in the business world that I used to help me with my area meetings. One was to start meetings on time. Officials were giving of themselves enough time coming to these meetings that it wasn't doing anyone any good to wait for 10-15 minutes for any latecomers before starting the meeting. The other was that we could discuss all the issues and rulings we wanted, but just listening to me wasn't going to make sure everyone would remember. So I made sure to put an agenda together for each meeting. We had plenty of things to discuss, but never had hard copies of any agendas to go over with those in attendance.

Paul actually let me come by the office and make copies to hand out at each meeting. I am a visual learner and having a written agenda helped me keep the meetings on track and gave those who came something to take home and review or discuss after it was over. So if someone had a question about something at the meeting, they could just look back at the agenda and see what was discussed. I included rule references, quiz questions, and casebook plays.

Honestly, it also made me a much better official. Since I spent so much time putting the agenda together and making sure to include everything the association wanted to see discussed, it made me spend so much more time in the rule book. At the end of this chapter is a copy of one of my agendas for an Area Meeting I from the 2003-04 basketball season.

There were two things that I wanted everyone to know when each meeting started. One was that I was not the area supervisor because I was the best official or that I knew all the rules. Far from it. I was corrected on more than one occasion. I was the area supervisor because the activities association trusted me to deliver the information to officials that they felt was needed during the year. The second thing was listed at the top of each agenda about the purpose of area meetings straight out of the KSHSAA official's handbook. So that what happened at each meeting wasn't just something I dreamed up, but what the association's expectations were for these meetings.

It turned out to be a really good opportunity for me. Paul liked my agendas and soon after the season was over, the director of football, Rick Bowden, called to offer me the football responsibilities as well. I accepted those as well.

For the next 10 years I conducted all the meetings for both Uncle Rick for football and Uncle Paul for basketball. It also gave me some other opportunities with the activities association. I was able to participate with a group known in Kansas as the Officials Policy Review Committee. This group helps provide some direction to the association regarding issues impacting all officials. Everything from hosting responsibilities of schools, to pay, to league commissioners, to the selection of post-season officials. I also was elected to the activities association Board of Directors and eventually on their Executive Board, which oversaw everything regarding the association and their member schools.

Outside of officiating, my time serving the activities association was sometimes more rewarding than officiating. It really was a great opportunity to serve with others who I felt carried the same ideals I had for high school activities. I remain very grateful for Paul and all of those at the association for the trust they gave me to represent them at so many different levels. It is just too bad that all officials don't have the same opportunity to see what it looks like from their side.

KSHSAA AREA MEETING #1
DECEMBER 2 – LAWRENCE, DECEMBER 3 – TOPEKA

I. Introductions

II. **"The purpose of these meetings is to achieve a more uniform application, understanding and interpretation by registered officials of the rules that apply to the sport they officiate and the mechanics of officiating." (KSHSAA Officials Handbook)**
   A. Consistency
   B. Improvement of Mechanics
   C. Continued Training
   D. Development of a positive attitude

III. 2003-2004 Rule Changes
   A. Warning signal for replacing a disqualified player added (2-12-5)
      -3-3-1c Exception; Simplified and Illustrated, Page 15
   B. Expanded definition of basket interference (4-6-4; 9-11-4)
   C. Point-differential rule established (5-5-3 note; Basketball Announcement Sheet)
   D. Number of lane-line players reduced for free throws (8-1-3)
   E. Direct technical foul assessed to the head coach after permitting a player to participate after being disqualified. (This is not the same as a player participating in too many quarters.) (10-5-3)

IV. Editorial Changes
   A. Bench Area Defined (1-13-3)
   B. Defensive Match up Request (3-3-1e)
   C. Knee and ankle braces clarified (3-5-1)
   D. Establishing legal guarding position (4-23) (Handout)
   E. Timeout charged when no correction made (5-11-3)
   F. Simultaneous foul throw-in spot (7-5-9 note)

V. Points of Emphasis
   A. Sporting Behavior
   B. Rough Play (Handout)
   C. Free Throw Administration
   D. Time Out Administration
   E. Substituting Player Disqualifications

F. End of Game Situations – Intentional Fouls

VI. New Signals and Mechanic Changes
   A. End of First Half (109a)
   B. Disqualified Player Notification (118)
   C. "Bird Dog" for Clarification only (230b; 240b)
   D. Lead's Ball-Side Coverage (Two-Person) (204)
   E. Time-Out/Intermission Positions (273; 275)
   F. Primary Court Coverage (Three-Person)
   G. Lead Initiates Rotation (314a)
   H. No Long Switch Eliminated (343)

VII. Integrity & Professionalism
   A. Contracts/Commissioners/Assignments
   B. Contact the school and your partners. . . at any level!!!
   C. No switches w/o approval
   D. Conduct a pre-game meeting
   E. Officials Quarterly handout

VIII. Questions on test.

IX. **O**fficials **P**olicy **R**eview **C**ommittee (Handout)

X. Adjourn

Dates to remember:

Series 2 Meetings:	**January 7, 2004 – Lawrence**
	January 14, 2004 – Topeka
Post-Season Application:	**January 30, 2004**
Series 3 Meetings:	**February 4, 2004 – Topeka**
	February 5, 2004 Lawrence

"305"

As I have mentioned, for most of my officiating career, I worked three sports, football, basketball, and baseball. Those three can take a toll on an official's body. Fields with decent grass and in good condition can certainly help an official, especially if it multiple games and long, hot days are involved.

Each sport has its own physical demands. Football, with its 100-yard field, can make for some long sprinting runs. Also, with 22 players on the field and that many, or more, on each sideline, officials never seem to completely avoid contact. And sometimes that contact can be serious. Ask football umpires or wing officials.

Basketball, though an indoor sport, could be the most physically demanding of the three I worked. The constant running back and forth, the quick change of direction, the fact that no one can run faster than the ball can be passed down the court.

Early on in my basketball career, I had my sister go with me to track just how much running I did during a game. This night I was working a girls and boys varsity doubleheader. She sat in the stands and made a mark every time I crossed mid court. And this was back in the day when we were all still working basketball games with two officials.

My idea being that from the end line to the 28 foot mark at the other end of the court was 56 feet on this 84 foot court. All told, between the two games I crossed the mid court line over 300 times. Okay, some might have been walking to the other end of the floor for free throws. Or some trips might have been shortened due to turnovers or other game situations. But in the long run, it should all even out. 300 trips at 60 feet per trip equal 18,000 feet. Other words, over three miles!

Do that three, four, sometimes five nights each week for three months and the miles begin to add up. Then do that for over 35 years. It soon begins to take its toll.

As for baseball, the physical demands are so much different. Yes, the up and down behind the plate can be taxing.

But most umpires really don't notice it until after the game is over. An umpire's concentration and focus behind the plate is on so many other things, that very rarely does an umpire pick up on how tiring it can become. And working the bases brings its own set of demands. When baseball games last two or three hours, that is when a base umpire begins to feel it the most in their feet and legs. That is why, given the opportunity, I would just a soon work the plate as the bases.

Given all that, I would not trade the 30 plus years of working the three sports year after year. Yes, there were days when I got home late and it would take me a couple of hours to wind down before I could go to sleep. There were times when I didn't feel like going to work the next day, or going to the next game.

Along with the occasional aches and pains there were the sprained ankles, the foul balls that hit you where you weren't protected, the knock downs and stepped on from would be tacklers. The standing out in the rain or snow in football. The twice-as-long trips home from a basketball game after the snowstorm hit while you were inside working. The waiting the now-customary 30 minutes after the last flash of lightening or sound of thunder for teams to return to the baseball field.

One year, during basketball season, I sprained the same ankle twice within one week. Another year, I strained an Achilles during a college game before getting a few days off when a snow storm hit to cancel games for a while. I have a whole suitcase full of medical apparatuses that I have worn off and on for my feet, ankles, knees, and arms. To go along with that are the tubes and bottles of ointments and pain killers just to get you through the next couple of hours.

And, yes, I have been banged up to the point that I probably should not have worked that next game; running on a leg that was probably not much better than 50 percent; fighting a cold or something else that you haven't been able to shake for days.

Remember when I said earlier that I always drive? The lone exception was the one time my wife drove home to Lyons from Concordia after a basketball game at Cloud County Community College. My guess it was the flu. Usually, I would work the game and at some point while sweating, my body would seem to rid itself of whatever virus was working on me at the time. Well, this time I felt so much worse after the game than before that I asked her to drive.   Boy, she knew then I didn't feel very well.

About 30 miles outside of Concordia, I made her pull over and to the ditch I went to get rid of whatever it was that wanted so much to get out of my stomach. I was so bad that I wound up calling a replacement for me the next night back in Concordia. You can count on both hands the number of games I have turned back for any reason.

In the end, health is a big factor for any official. And I have tried every over-the-counter remedy known to man at one time of another. At this time, the ointment of choice is Bio-freeze, if it is muscle related, or Volteran Gel, if it is joint related. Then the usual dose of Ibuprofen and Tylenol.

I am also not afraid to use a chiropractor. When I was really busy with the three sports, it was not unusually for me to stop in and see my chiropractor at the beginning of each new season. Despite being very active with each sport, each demanded a difference use of muscles. And the first time or two with each left me just a little tighter than before. My chiropractor in Topeka was really good and very informed about sports and sports injuries. His wife was actually an assistant high school golf coach with Jeff Stromgren. He said Jeff was in about every couple of weeks during the basketball season. So I really didn't feel so bad about seeing him three or four times during the year.

But, knock on wood, there were very few times that my officiating sent me to seek any real serious medical care. Like everyone else, I did need to see my doctor for a variety of health issues, including the always present winter season colds and assorted viruses.

One such trip was to my personal physician in February with one of those head colds that stood out and really knocked me for a loop. It caused me to finally decide to do something to take better stock in my personal health.

As is standard practice when one sees their physician, the nurse calls your name and as you head down the hall to the examination room, the nurse asks you step on the scale. And as always, I did. The next thing I heard is the title of this chapter. I don't know what I thought I weighed, but that number I heard that day really smacked me upside the head.

I got my checkup and my prescription for my Z-pack, but I was still thinking about what I heard the nurse say. It was about a 20-minute drive home and during that time the only thing I could think of was that I don't know what I am going to do, but I have to do something. When I got home, I discussed my thoughts with my wife. One thing I knew I was going to do was wait until we got home from a cruise we were planning to take after the current basketball season was over. So I had basically a month to figure it out and put a plan in place.

In the meantime, all I could think about was how was I still getting any games, anywhere, for anything. Then I thought just how much better I would be if I weighed a lot less.

After getting home from our cruise in late March, I had made the decision to work with a nutrition and weight loss physician in Topeka who I had heard about and had talked to others who had used him as well. I also had in my mind that I wanted to lose 65 pounds.

The program basically consisted of a high protein, low carb diet consisting of some specialty foods from the physician and some specially selected foods from the store. Gone were the regular soda, fast food, and my ever pleasing milk. Even though I had switched to a low-fat milk some time before, what I found out was based on what my caloric intake was, over half of it consisted of liquids. I have always loved milk and would generally go through a gallon about every couple of days. It was not unusual for me to come home some days thirsty and knock down close to a half gallon of milk right there.

I found out that sugar free Jell-O was a "free food", as was salsa, dill pickles, and of course water. The whole idea centered on eating six times each day, Breakfast, mid-morning snack, lunch, mid-afternoon snack, dinner, and evening snack. I checked in with the physician every week. His office guaranteed me that I would lose five pounds the first week. I lost 10.

In six months, I lost the 65 pounds I had set as my goal. Obviously, none of my clothes fit me anymore, including my officiating clothes. I had continued to wear my 48-waist pants through that spring's baseball season, even though my belt needed some new notches. That high school all-star basketball game that I drove nearly 500 miles round trip for was coming up in August which forced me to find some new slacks for basketball.

After stepping away from the program, my next year of officiating might have been the one I look forward to the most in nearly 20 years. I was amazed at how well I moved and how well I felt. I eventually found a balance with my diet and have held pretty steady going on nearly 15 years now. Yes, I have gained some back. But I can go into about any store now and find clothes without having to look specifically in the big and tall section.

I'm a regular scale watcher (I hear that is not ideal, but it works for me); I use a fitness app that helps me count calories; I keep track of my blood pressure; and I get a regular yearly physical. I do still fight pre-diabetes, (a family history), high blood pressure, and Oreos. Both my parents passed away at the age of 57. Both from stroke related issues. The year of my 57th birthday was a nervous year for me. That has been a few years ago now.

Is my diet perfect? No. But I do try and watch what I eat. My wife is a great cook and I do love to eat. Actually, my officiating schedule was a blessing; otherwise there is no telling what that scale might have said that day in the doctor's office. I remain active outside of officiating and I am a lot more cognizant of my health now than I was that day.

Who knows, as long as they keep making Bio freeze, Volteren Gel, and Ibuprofen, there might still be a need for an old, slow, but less heavy official.

A FINAL MOVE?

Very few officials get to dictate where they live. Obviously, those in the professional leagues may have that opportunity. Some major league umpires look towards the warmer climates for their off season.

But most of us who work high school and college sports also have to have a full-time occupation that pays the bills. For most of us, the money we make from officiating helps with vacations, extras around the house, emergency funds, or things for our family. A few major college basketball officials have used their avocation as their primary occupation, but they really are few and far between.

My move from Lyons to Topeka was related to my job and not for officiating reasons. As I mentioned before, though that move was within the same state (Kansas), it was almost like starting over again. New schedules, new schools, new partners, just a different environment.

But, my wife and I spent some time looking after my mother-in-law. We moved her down from Minnesota to be near us in Topeka. When she passed in 2009, we were ready for our next adventure. We began to explore other options and potential locations.

We were very interested in what Arizona had to offer. Phoenix was where we spent our honeymoon. We continued to visit the area off and on for a variety of reasons, most notably the warmer winter weather. We also remained close to my wife's side of the family and had made regular holiday trips to Colorado through the years.

Ultimately, we decided that we were not ready to spend the summer in Arizona. (Yes, we know, it's a dry heat!) So we continued to focus on Colorado, and specifically, Colorado Springs. But there was no definitive timetable and no real urgency driving this decision other than a home we thought we would enjoy.

Then in July 2011, while in Colorado Springs, we found it. I was in town volunteering for the USGA US Men's Senior Open at the Broadmoor. In between those responsibilities we spent our time looking at house after house. We knew it when we came across it. We got all of our ducks in a row during that time and set it up to close on the house in August.

Even though we had been working on this for nearly two years, it was still a pretty sudden decision as far as Topeka was concerned. We had a house that needed packed up, we needed movers, and we needed to pin down the entire schedule and what that was going to look like over the next several weeks. We had a trip to Iowa scheduled that wound up being right between the time we closed on our house in Colorado and when the movers would ultimately be able to deliver our goods. So basically, we had three weeks to get our you-know-what together.

As far as my officiating was concerned, things needed to move just as fast as well. I did work a few more baseball games in Topeka that July. But there were some other, timelier, officiating decisions that needed to be made.

At this point, our football crew had our 2011 football schedule. Along with me now moving, there were also a couple of earlier changes to our crew. Thankfully, the one veteran crew member remaining, who knew this could happen, took over the crew, its schedule, and its new crew members. And these were not just new crew members, but fairly new football officials as well.

We had decided during the off-season, to bring on some new, younger officials for the upcoming year. We are talking about guys in their early 20's who, we felt, were ready to be up and coming officials. On a side note, as of 2017, one of these guys is now working college football, one is also working major college baseball, and another one has moved up to Triple A baseball. Needless to say, I hated dumping this on one of my partners. But, as it turned out, he stepped up and got through the season, and has continued to oversee the crew, even now.

My other, timelier, officiating issue was my duties as the football and basketball area supervisor for the activities association. Again, this is something that they knew was on our plate, but we had continued to move forward with me and these duties. At this point, they basically had a month to find a new area supervisor. It was their feeling that they wanted to continue with someone currently working both sports. In time they did find someone, who continues to hold down both positions today.

My final logistical hurdle to take care of from Kansas were my two basketball tournaments that I had worked for more than 20 years, the Hays City Shootout in early December and the Tournament of Champions in Dodge City in January. These tournaments had been a part of me and my basketball schedule since before my move to Topeka. So I wanted to keep these on my schedule, as least for the immediate future. As it turned out, they were both as interested in keeping me on as well. The reality of it was, being in Colorado Springs was only about 20 miles further from Dodge City than Topeka.

So after getting all my T's crossed and my I's dotted in Kansas, I now had to figure out where and how officiating worked in Colorado. As it turned out, I did have a contact in the activities association office there. A few years earlier, I made a presentation to a group of state activities association staff from the Midwest at a summit that was hosted by the Kansas office in Topeka. At that meeting was Tom Robinson from Colorado. Tom oversaw officiating in Colorado and worked for the state office as a liaison to the officials organizations in the state.

So Tom put me in touch with basketball contacts in Colorado Springs. With the time of the move, I knew that football was going to be out of the question, but that basketball would work for the upcoming year. With baseball in the spring, there would be more than enough time to work on that, especially after getting my feet wet with basketball.

As it turned out, the new official's classes that I needed to go through would begin in September. Obviously, I was not a new official, but this would not be the only thing that I would have to get used to in moving to a new state. After over 30 years in Kansas, the officiating structure for all sports in Colorado, I found, was completely different.

In Colorado, the state oversees officiating, but it is the local organizations that actually administer and carry out all training, instruction, and scheduling. And each sport operates and registers its officials independently. Working three sports also meant three different registrations dates. It also meant that I went from paying $46 for three sports in Kansas, to paying $315 in Colorado.

Basketball in Colorado also introduced me to IAABO (International Association of Amateur Basketball Officials). High school officials in Colorado have chosen to follow IAABO's guidelines regarding mechanics and training. Primarily an organization found on the east coast, Colorado is a 100 percent state with IAABO, so joining was not an option. The actual mechanics were not that much different. The only real mechanic change was where the calling official was to go. In Federation mechanics, the calling official at the time would stay table-side as the trail in three-person mechanics. In IAABO, the calling official would go back across the floor, to the center position, like college men mechanics. It did take some getting used to, then just about the time I got comfortable with that, I had to go back to Kansas for either the Hays Shootout or Tournament of Champions and remember to change again.

Football and baseball were all Federation mechanics and rules in Colorado. But there were definitely some differences in the structure and training for each sport.

In Kansas, I worked with the same football crew for all my nearly 20 years in Topeka. You put a crew of five together and you put a schedule together and you worked your games. If crew members left, you found replacements for the next year and beyond. In Colorado, the crew consists of 12-14 members, all selected through a crew draft held in the spring by all the crew chiefs, which were 8-10 in number in Colorado Springs.

It was up to each crew chief to assign games for the members of his crew. Each crew's schedule is put together by a local assigner with each crew chief picking his schedule out of a hat. Each schedule would include 14-16 varsity games with 40-50 other games, (i.e. sub-varsity, freshman, or middle school). Some Friday nights, a crew might have two varsity games, which meant that 10 officials were needed to fill those slots.

It would be possible for crews to substitute if need be from a "sister crew". These sister crews were used to help fill needed positions, as well as get together for smaller meetings between the required full association meetings. Each year could mean a completely new crew, maybe even a new position. I was a member of five different crews during my time in Colorado. For each, I was able to spend most of my time working as a Referee, or "White Hat" each year. But I have spent some time at other positions as well.

There are pros and cons to each system. Colorado definitely does help a new official. New officials will find themselves with other officials with whom they can work together. They don't have to worry about when or where they will work games, or trying to sell themselves in an effort to find a crew.

But there was some comfort in Kansas being able to work season after season with the same five guys. You get to know their habits, their strengths, their weaknesses. You ride together every week. You find common interests outside of football.

A more notable change for me in 2012 in Colorado was with the uniform. No more knickers, though Kansas has since moved away from them as well. No narrow striped shirt, though in 2017, Kansas provided that as an option for officials. And the availability of wearing shorts for non-varsity contests. Though, for me, that was a change I was slow to get comfortable with. In no other sport that we work, does the uniform change for officials when the level of play changes. Not basketball, not baseball. However, on a side note, while watching a show on NFL Network about Doug Flutie, I did see officials in shorts when Boston College went to South Carolina to play Clemson in 1982.

My baseball did come a little easier. Though I was obligated to work my fill of high school sub-varsity contests that first year in Colorado, it was an easy transition to a full high school varsity schedule. I also was able to step in and work some college baseball in Colorado. Though not as plentiful as Kansas, (30 colleges compared to 10) college baseball games in Colorado, did provide me an opportunity to reconnect with some coaches with Midwest roots from Kansas and Missouri.

Eventually, I was able to work some post-season games in each sport. And I was able to help in other ways as well, including working as an observer for both high school football and high school basketball during the post-season and helping with instruction during the high school baseball season at regular association meetings.

But, since this time, there has been another move that has presented additional challenges. Remember when I said my wife and I were looking at both Arizona and Colorado when the time came to look beyond Kansas? Well, Arizona never completely left our minds. And just recently, we did go ahead and purchase another home in Sun City West, Arizona, in the West Valley of Phoenix, near the Surprise and Peoria area. So, now being "snowbirds", I find myself working high school baseball in my third state.

Though I have spent nearly 40 years working baseball, again Arizona saw me as a first-year official. This time however, I was able to work in Arizona as a reciprocal official, using my current registration from Colorado. I did need to attend new official's classes. As a transfer, I was also required to attend and work at a "move-up" scrimmage where officials are evaluated for an opportunity to move up through the 1-5 ranking system used to place officials. With 1 being the top level for officials through 4 for first-year officials, with 5 being used for transfer officials. My three innings of work at the scrimmage allowed me to move from a 5 to a 1 that first season.

And a new state meant another new system to navigate. The pre-season meeting for all umpires in the Phoenix metro area was held at Chase Field, home of the Arizona Diamondbacks. All local meetings were actually held during the pre-season. With games on every day of the week, and with the number of schools in the metro area, and with the ever-present shortage of umpires, meeting during the season would just take away from the already short number of umpires on the field.

That first season went fairly well. There are some quality teams in the Phoenix area, but there also were some that resemble just about every other team on the lower end of the quality scale. I was able to work a full varsity schedule, as full as the schedule could be with two days dedicated to playing softball and two days dedicated to playing golf.

Overall, I was pleased with the games I got and with the overall quality of partners available. With just a few exceptions, the quality of the playing fields in Arizona is outstanding for high school baseball. But that is probably what you should expect when you can grow grass 365 days out of the year. I will certainly look forward to going back for additional seasons.

I can only hope that there will not be any further moves in my future. Obviously, no one knows for sure, but it is nice knowing that a qualified official can find work just about anywhere he or she goes.

IT'S GOING TO COME TO AN END SOMETIME

No one can go on forever. Especially officials. All the greats had to hang it up sooner or later. Jim Tunney, Ben Dreith, Jerry Markbreit, Hank Nichols, Mendy Rudolph, Earl Strom, Joe Crawford, Shag Crawford, Harry Wendelstedt, even John Deedrick. Father Time is undefeated.

For some it is age, for some it is injury, for some it is a lifestyle change. For others, it could be family responsibilities, or job commitments, or a change in location. But, sooner or later, it's going to come to an end.

For many like me, when we started this journey, we had goals and aspirations for what we wanted our officiating career to look like; where we wanted it to take us, what games we wanted to work, who we wanted to get in front of.

Each official has his or her own set of goals and interests. Some wish to ascend to the professional ranks in their particular sport, others are just looking for some extra money. Some want to give back to their sport of choice. Some wish to work high school varsity, while others wish to advance to the college ranks.

When I started out, some of us talked how we couldn't see ourselves still working high school games as we neared social security age. Some of us could not see ourselves still working at all 30-40 years down the road. I personally, had no definite end game in mind.

Obviously, when I started, I wanted my officiating career to take me wherever it could. When I started, I wanted to advance to high school varsity games. When I received high school varsity games, I was interested in advancing to college games. I admit that when I started getting college basketball games, I did put in an inquiry with the CBA, (now the NBA G League) but never seriously pursued it.

Eventually, things settled down and most of my officiating career centered on high school varsity contests for football and basketball, with a baseball schedule filled with mostly college games. At least until we moved to Colorado. The Colorado move required me to take a step back, as did our latest move to Arizona for the winter.

For most officials, health is a top factor in maintaining a schedule. It may not be the only factor, but it probably has the most influence on an officials' decision to continue or not.

I mentioned a couple of health issues with my officiating career earlier. Believe me there have been many others. Just about every sport requires an official to be on his or her feet. Most of those also require an official to move from one end of the playing surface to the other. That means the feet, knees, and legs can really take a pounding year after year. It soon became apparent to me that as I got a year older, the high school and college participants got a year younger.

I have no doubt that there were some nights and days that I should not have been on the court, field, or diamond. It could have been something as minor as a cold, or something more physically serious.

Due to two severely flat feet, compliments of my parents, feet have always been a priority of mine. Every couple of seasons meant a new pair of officiating shoes and new insoles. Even today, the first thing I do when I get a new pair of athletic shoes is take out the insoles that come with those shoes and replace them with an insole specifically designed for athletic shoes. Besides the shoes, came new socks and tights for my legs. Starting in high school as an athlete, I have been adamant in wearing two pair of socks.

No one style or brand of shoe was necessary as styles and quality continued to change over the years. Converse, Adidas, Reebok, Avia, Puma, you name it. Thankfully, I did come along after the old-style ribbed Spotbilt coaches shoes were the shoe of choice for most officials, regardless of the sport.

But at some point near my 50th birthday, the issues started to become more severe and more frequent. Some requiring more care than just ice packs and tape. And though my dad was an athlete and active, my family history was not doing me any favors.

I've worked with several officials who looked like they were going to play and not officiate. Between the tape and the wraps and braces and assorted ointments, you would be surprised that they could even move. Some even referred to it as going to war. Sometimes, I wondered the same thing myself.

There were the sprained ankles and the tired achy feet. There were the sore leg muscles. There were the short nights with little sleep. The bruises from the foul balls that made it difficult to work the indicator. And there were those times when I could not answer the bell. Thankfully, they were few and far between, but some of that was due to a wiser approach to my schedule and the ability to ultimately recognize my own limitations.

The first such serious issue came during early January of the 2000-2001 basketball season. It happened during a college men's game on a Monday night at McPherson College. At some point just before halftime, I felt the strong pull in the lower part of my left leg, near my ankle. I mentioned it at halftime to my partners and found myself nursing it through the second half, finally getting to the end. With a high school game the next night I did ice it on the way home and took care not to do too much on it the next day, before my high school doubleheader that next night.

One saving grace for me that next night was that we were going to be playing on a 74 ft. high school court. One of the few left, in Kansas, and probably the country as well. Another welcomed sight was that the girl's game turned into a blowout with coaches agreeing to shorten the final two quarters. I have no doubt that my less than agile gait was noticeable to most in attendance. (Remember, I said there were some nights when I should not have been on the court?!)

I was able to get in and see my primary care physician the next day. The ultimate diagnosis was a strained Achilles. He said I was not in any more danger of doing any more damage

138

than I had already done. So basically, I could do anything on it that I could tolerate, which meant I could try and officiate.

I did work another girls/boys doubleheader on Friday night. Then luck came to my defense. The following week was the Tournament of Champions in Dodge City. Six boys games over three days on Thursday, Friday, and Saturday. As it turned out, we got hit with some severe winter weather on Monday and Tuesday of that week, that canceled my games heading into that weekend. That, in turn, gave me six days to get it back into some kind of shape heading to Dodge City.

This wasn't the only time I headed into the tournament in Dodge City with some concern regarding my ability to get up and down the floor. Knees, ankles, tight muscles in the lower back, hamstrings, they all were an issue at one time or another. A couple of things worked in my favor. One, I loved working on that floor in the old Civic Center in Dodge City. Despite there being concrete right off the edge of the floor, the floor itself felt really good to my feet and legs. The other factor was that Dodge City had a full-time athletic trainer who was as good as any doctor I could have seen. He spent as much, if not more, time taking care of the six officials that week than he did with eight basketball teams.

Other serious issues have made their presence known through the years; not the least of which were potential blood clots in my left leg prior to one of my last football seasons in Kansas. My doctor said being it was in a superficial vein, he did not consider it to be serious. He had a hard time convincing my wife and me of that. This would not be the last time this issue came up.

Then there were the injuries incurred during a contest. Sprained ankles, hands hit by foul balls, toes stepped on by would-be tacklers. But nothing would prepare me for the one night at the NBC tournament.

I happened to be behind the plate late that night. Despite all the precaution umpires take to protect themselves, there is always that one ball that gets through. I cannot recall exactly

139

where in the game it occurred. But the short and sweet of it goes like this; pitch comes in, low and in the dirt, bounces under the catcher and catches me right between the legs.

Yes, I (we) wear protection there. Yes, it hit me in my protection. Yes, it hurt . . . a lot! Yes, I went to my knees. Yes, I stayed on my knees for some time. Yes, the catcher was very apologetic. Yes, my brother, who was in the stands that night, threatened to come down and kick the catcher's ass.

After what seemed like a very long time, we resumed the game without any further injury. But I was damn sore after the game. I also had a two-hour drive ahead of me that night back to Topeka from Wichita. Thankfully, my wife was along to keep my company.

Not thinking too much about it on the way home, we arrived in Topeka sometime after midnight. As I stopped the car and started to get out after parking in the garage, I knew right then, getting into the house was going to be difficult to say the least. Basically, I could barely move. And my injured parts had swollen to about four times their normal size. And that was even after ice had been applied on the ride home.

It took the better part of the next day before I could feel like things were returning the normal. But I was pretty jumpy back there for the next few games.

But age and wear and tear really did catch up with me during the summer of 2013. It happened on a baseball field in Cheyenne, Wyoming. I cannot tell you when, where, or how. But I can tell you that the next morning, my left foot was so sore and stiff that I could barely walk out to the car in the hotel parking lot. I had another game that night and it did loosen up some during the day for me, which included a trip to the Cheyenne Frontier Days Rodeo that afternoon.

I fussed with this for the next several weeks, going into the fall and the football season. Eventually, as football wound down, I needed to find out what was going on. My annual physical was coming up prior to basketball season, so it was a good time to inquire with my primary physician what I needed to do next. My primary physician sent me to a podiatrist. After x-rays and an exam, the podiatrist diagnosed that I had a posterior tibial tendon that had given out in my foot.

The posterior tibial tendon attaches the calf muscle to the bones on the inside of the foot. The main function of this tendon is to hold up the arch and support the foot when walking. As I mentioned before, I really have no arch in my feet. So for all these years, this tendon was doing the work of supporting an arch that wasn't there until it finally said enough. The podiatrist wanted to do surgery right away. Hold on there cowboy! I had a basketball season to get through.

I scheduled a second opinion with an orthopedic surgeon who was a foot and ankle specialist and who also worked with the United States Olympic Training Center in Colorado Springs. It took him all of about five minutes to confirm the previous diagnosis. After telling him I was sure that surgery was going to be in my future, my immediate goal was to get through what I knew was going to be my 35th and final basketball season.

He assured me we could do that, but not without some assistance. That came in the form of a walking boot that I was to wear just about any time I was not officiating. I wore it to many games, including my last trip to Dodge City. I also was on a steady diet of pain medication, not all of it over-the-counter.

Long story short, I finished the basketball season. Though I tried to work the following baseball season, I finally gave in and shut things down and eventually had surgery in July, 2014. The delay was due to an effort to get my vitamin D up to a level that my orthopedic surgeon felt would be beneficial in my recovery. Ultimately, the surgeon put in three 4-inch screws in my foot/ankle, basically building me an arch. I also suffered from the before-mentioned blood clots as a result of the surgery. I eventually was laid up from officiating for 15 months.

This was also the same year that I turned that previously mentioned 57. Needless to say, I spent a lot of time looking in the mirror and recounting all my health concerns.

I had a follow-up procedure the following summer to remove one of the screws and clean up some scar tissue which helped greatly. It took basically two years to feel like I had fully recovered enough to give a quality effort in getting back to working football and baseball again.

Below is my x-ray after the original procedure in 2014.

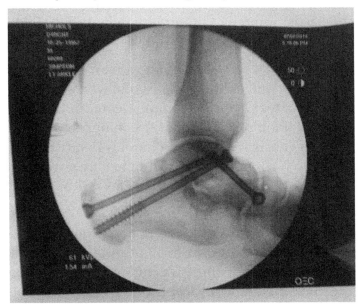

I eventually got back to some post-season assignments in football and found myself back working a state baseball semi-final game in Colorado. In addition, I had gotten involved with Little League baseball in Colorado. Little League gave me the opportunity to work state championships in Colorado and regional tournaments in Albuquerque, New Mexico and Seguin, Texas. Ultimately, I found myself earning a Junior League (13-14 year olds) World Series assignment in Taylor, Michigan in 2016. I was lucky enough to work first base during the championship game, televised on ESPN, won by Chinese Taipei 9-1 over Hawaii.

Beyond that, I have been blessed with the type and quality of games that I have worked. I worked four NBC championship games over the years, including the championship game on the plate in which a bunch of former pro's from Midlothian, Illinois made a statement with 21 runs and 7 home runs in the last championship game played with metal bats. I was also awarded the NBC Umpire of the Year in 2001.

I worked a state championship basketball game in Kansas and several championship finals in both the Hays City Shootout and the Tournament of Champions. I've worked high school state baseball tournaments in Kansas, Colorado and Arizona. I have also worked high school state football playoffs in both Kansas and Colorado.

I got my opportunity to work college basketball at both the men's and women's level, including post-season games on both sides. I got plenty of opportunities to work college baseball all across Kansas and Missouri at the junior college, NAIA, and NCAA Division II level. I even got my turn at some non-conference baseball games at the Division I level at Wichita State, Kansas State, and the University of Kansas, and a ton of quality summer baseball in the Jayhawk League. I worked one of the final AIAW college women's softball regionals in Lawrence, Kansas right before the NCAA took over administration of women's sports.

Across the state of Kansas, I covered everything in all four corners. In Goodland (Northwest) I worked the Topside Classic in high school basketball. In Pittsburg (Southeast) I worked college baseball. In Liberal (Southwest) I worked college basketball. And in Elwood (Northeast) I worked high school football.

I have been on the floor or the field with some well-known names. Adrian Griffin, Josh Reid, Jordy Nelson, Jackie Stiles, Brandy Perryman, Darren Driefort, the 1996 USA Olympic Baseball team, Todd Tichenor, Gary Woodland, Ron Baker, Semi Ojeleye, and Christian McCaffrey.

That ankle/foot hasn't been the last major health setback. Other health issues have come to light recently that have me thinking about my life beyond officiating, especially now that we have moved into full retirement with homes in two different states. And my golf game has seen some level of improvement as well. (Courses in Arizona have a way of doing that!)

Then there are also three little boys in our lives now, Hunter, Liam, and Quinn that keep Nana and Papa hopping. At this time, they are 7-year-old identical triplet boys who can't seem to get enough of us. Or us of them, we are not sure which. They have seen Papa work games in all three sports. They went with us to those basketball tournaments in Hays and Dodge City. We even took them back to Sterling for the Fourth of July celebration. Maybe I can pass on some officiating talents to one of them.

Whether this ends within the next few months or next few years, it has been a great trip. Officiating introduced me to some great people, allowed me to see some great places and be in the middle of the action in some games that I could have only dreamed about at one time. The avocation has been very good to me and for me. I was lucky enough to get started at an early age and find my way some 40 plus years later. It is hard for me to believe that there was a time when it seemed only officiating mattered. Now, I find it hard to believe it doesn't matter as much.

I know lots of officials who get started at a later age only to wish they would have started sooner. If anyone out there has any questions about whether they, or anyone, should consider getting involved in officiating, I have only one thing to say to you.

Would I do it all over? Absolutely!

THANKS!

The names listed here are those who, in one way or another, have been an influence to my career as an official. It all began during that summer in 1973. And along the way, these are some of those people who helped me grow and sustain my officiating career. There are many names on this list that are no longer with us. This list includes officials, assigners, coaches, athletic directors, administrators, and those who looked the other way when I went missing from work from time to time. There are going to be many names that even my closest officiating friends are not going to know, or even know why they are on this list.

There are names on this list that others have had some conflict with, people who they cannot stand. That is fine with me. I can only say that I became the official and the person I am, in large part to the names you see on the next page.

We all have special people that have impacted our lives every day. My listing their names here is my small way to say thank you for putting up with me, my questions, my desires, and my willingness to learn and teach. I have no doubt that someone is missed. To each of you, I offer my most sincere thanks for everything you have done for me.

Harold Adams
Bruce Andrews
Bert Borgmann
Rick Bowden
Don Butts
Randy Campbell
Alan Clark
Todd Clark
John Dabrow
John Deedrick
George Demetriou
Leonard Detter
Bruce Dinkle
Brian Embery
Dennis Erkenbrack
Richard Gillenwaters
Clair Gleason
Jimmy Godfrey
Ken Harmon
Bruce Harper
Jerry Harris
Marion Heim
Tony Hobson
Bob Homolka
Mike Karl
Rick Keltner
Bill Klecan
Duane Koelsch
Larry Lady
Bennie Lee
Carl Lewton
Ray Lutz
Mark Lytle

Fran Martin
Kevin McClure
Jack Metzger
Curtis Miller
John Moore
Gary Musselmann
John Nelson
Clancy Norris
Kelly Nusser
Garlan Old
Paul Palmer
Kaye Pearce
Carlos Polk
Terry Pound
Wayne Prince
JC Riekenberg
Bob Shearer
JW Shirley
Frank Smysor
James Stapleton
Jerry Stremel
Jeff Stromgren
Don Strube
John Summerville
Duane Tidwell
Gary Tranbarger
Mark VanGampleare
Dennis Walker
Don Ward
Garrett Wheaton
Gary White
Ken Winkley
Fred Zercher

In addition, there are a couple of more people who need my attention. The first would be my father, Skip. He worked ASA softball back in the 60's, when they wore black shirts and black pants. I can remember my mom taking white shirts and dying them black with RIT dye on the stove. He worked a couple of state tournaments over his years. He helped some when I was playing youth league softball and was responsible for years for taking care of the softball diamond in Sterling. He introduced me to officiating. I would liked to have had his feedback as my officiating career moved along, but he passed away while I was still in college.

I also wish to acknowledge a couple of gentlemen who got me interested in writing. The first was Dr. Suhail Hanna, a former English Professor at Sterling College. His inter-term class of Introduction to Writing introduced me to my writing skills which later turned into a small part-time newspaper career in sports writing for my college paper, *The Sterling Stir*, and two local newspapers, *The Sterling Bulletin* and *The Lyons Daily News*.

And finally, John Sayler, the editor of the *Lyons Daily News*, who trusted me with sports stories, games articles, and a little bit of a free rein on Saturday mornings during the football and basketball seasons at the *Daily News*. From "Nick's Picks", to "From the Sidelines", to the Saturday morning calls to local high school coaches, I learned a lot about writing, telling the story, and meeting deadlines.

It has been a great trip. I hope you have enjoyed coming along with me.

95722640R00085

Made in the USA
Columbia, SC
20 May 2018